G000058378

REDISCOVERING MATHEMATICS

for the Caribbean

GRADE ONE

Dr. Adrian Mandara

LMH PUBLISHING LIMITED

Cover design: Sanya Dockery
Typeset & book layout: Sanya Dockery

Published by: LMH Publishing Limited
Suite 10-11
Sagicor Industrial Park
7 Norman Road
Kingston C.S.O., Jamaica
Tel.: (876) 938-0005; Fax: (876) 759-8752
Email: lmhbookpublishing@cwjamaica.com
Website: www.lmhpublishing.com

A Cataloguing-In-Publication data of this book is available at the National Library of Jamaica.

Printed in China

ISBN: 978-976-8245-87-8

PREFACE

Rediscovering Mathematics for the Caribbean is a series of books specially prepared for Caribbean schools. The texts are carefully planned and graded, with material covering kindergarten and classes in the primary schools.

The method of presentation and the materials used are in line with the modern trend of teaching mathematics. The topics are sound, up-to-date and relevant. The illustrations used are student-friendly and popular with children, and they help to convey the various concepts taught.

The student is asked to think very broadly, and many times a higher order of thinking is required. Topics are provided with adequate and varied exercises.

In order to develop the mathematical potential of the pupils to the fullest possible extent, it is hoped that the teacher will supplement each topic with similar, interesting mathematical activities. This will help the pupil to develop an awareness of the manifold applications of mathematics in almost every aspect of our modern world, and to gain enjoyment from mathematics.

Dedicated to the many students who strive to deepen their understanding of the subject.

CONTENTS

Counting Chart

1	2	3	4	5	6	7	8	9	10
11	12	13	14	15	16	17	18	19	20
21	22	23	24	25	26	27	28	29	30
31	32	33	34	35	36	37	38	39	40
41	42	43	44	45	46	47	48	49	50
51	52	53	54	55	56	57	58	59	60
61	62	63	64	65	66	67	68	69	70
71	72	73	74	75	76	77	78	79	80
81	82	83	84	85	86	87	88	89	90
91	92	93	94	95	96	97	98	99	100

VAMOS A CONTAR EN EL ESPAÑOL.

(Let's Count in Spanish)

uno		1
dos		2
tres		3
cuatro		4
cinco		5
seis		6
siete		7
ocho		8
nueve		9
diez		10

1	2	3	4	5	6	7	8	9	10
uno	dos	tres	cuatro	cinco	seis	siete	ocho	nueve	diez

I Can Count

Review of
NUMERALS AND THEIR NUMBER NAMES: 0 – 10

Study the numerals from zero to ten. The numerals zero to ten are:

0
zero

1
one

2
two

3
three

4
four

5
five

6
six

7
seven

8
eight

9
nine

10
ten

Hi, did you know that zero is the first whole number?

Fill in the missing numerals.

_____, 1, 2, 3, _____, _____, 6

2, 3, 4, 5, _____, _____, _____, 9

0, _____, _____, 3, 4, 5, 6, _____

_____, 4, 5, 6, _____, 8, _____

After zero comes one. After one comes two and so on. Numbers follow a pattern.

Which of the numerals does not belong?

Circle that numeral.

a.   0   1   2   3   9

b.   0   1   2   4   3

c.   4   5   9   6   7

d.   2   7   8   9   10

e.   5   6   8   7   3

This is a **number line** which shows the order of the numbers.

0 1 2 3 4 5 6 7 8 9 10

Draw a number line in your notebook.

The numbers that come in front are smaller. One comes in front of two. One is smaller than two.

Answer the questions below.

What number comes just before numeral 4? _____

What number comes just before numeral 2? _____

What number comes just before numeral 6? _____

What number comes just before numeral 10? _____

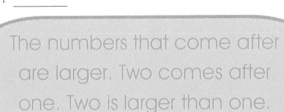

The numbers that come after are larger. Two comes after one. Two is larger than one.

Answer the questions below.

What number comes just after numeral 6? _____

What number comes just after numeral 3? _____

What number comes just after numeral 7? _____

What number comes just after numeral 0? _____

This is a number line which shows the order of the numbers.

Use the number line to answer the questions.

a. Which number comes just before one? _____

b. Which number comes just before ten? _____

c. The number that comes just before six is? _____

d. The number that comes just before nine is? _____

e. The number that comes just after two is? _____

f. The number that comes just after one is? _____

g. Which number comes just after five? _____

h. Which number comes just after nine? _____

Write the number names in reverse order from ten to five, in words.

Ten, _____, _____, _____, _____, five

Write the numerals in reverse order from ten to two?

10 ___, ___, ___, ___, ___, ___, ___, 2

Two comes before the number three. Two is one less than three.

Answer the questions below.

a.   What number is one less than six? _____

b.   What number is one less than one? _____

c.   What number is one less than five? _____

d.   What number is one less than nine? _____

Answer these questions.

If there were one less book, how many books would there be?

If there were one less football, how many footballs would there be?

_____

_____

If there were one less cat, how many cats would there be?

If there were one less apple, how many apples would there be?

_____

_____

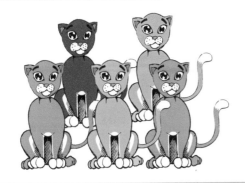

Count and connect the names in counting order.
What shape is formed?

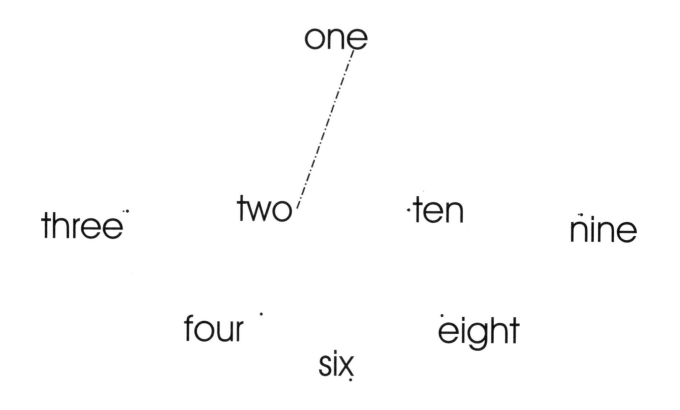

Count and colour the number of kites.

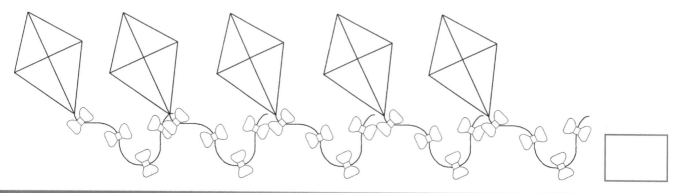

Ordinal Numbers

An ordinal number tells the position of a person or thing.

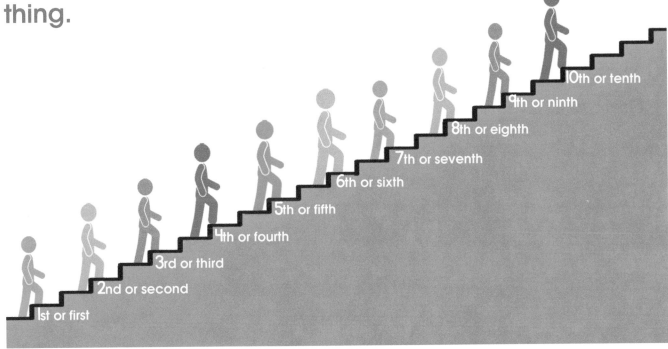

10th or tenth
9th or ninth
8th or eighth
7th or seventh
6th or sixth
5th or fifth
4th or fourth
3rd or third
2nd or second
1st or first

Number the students in the lunch line using ordinal numbers in their short forms. Put the short forms in the circle.

7

ORDINAL NUMBERS

Numbers that express order are ordinal numbers. They tell the position of a person or thing.

Example: First   Second   Third   Fourth   Fifth   Sixth

1st   2nd   3rd   4th   5th   6th

Mark an X on the third picture.

Mark an X on the 2nd picture.

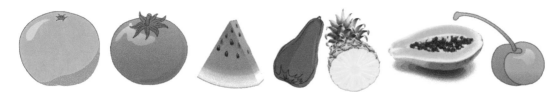

Mark an X on the 6th picture.

Ordinal numbers tell the position of a person or thing.

	1st	2nd	3rd
Example:			

Circle the third ball.

Underline the fifth star.

Circle the 4th turtle.

Underline the book in the first position.

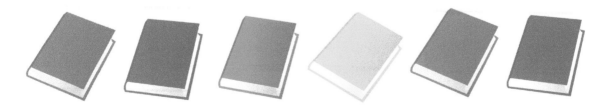

9

ORDINAL NUMBERS

Ordinal Numbers tell the position of an object or person.

Match the coloured object to the correct position.

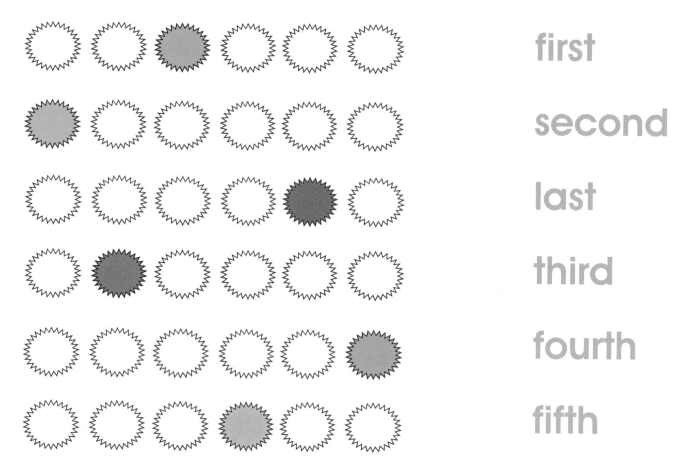

first

second

last

third

fourth

fifth

Circle the last object in each set.

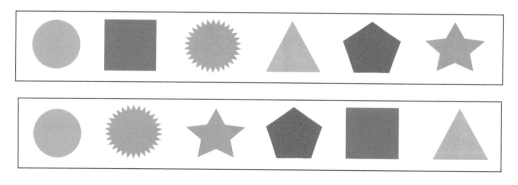

Ordinal numbers tell the position of a person or thing.

Example:

first   middle   last

Complete the sequence.

Here is an example.

<u>Third</u>   <u>Second</u>   First

Fifth   <u>Sixth</u>   Seventh

1. _____   _____   _____   Fourth

2. _____   Second   _____   _____

3. _____   _____   third   fourth   _____

ORDINAL NUMBERS

Write the ordinal number and its name for these numbers. The first one is done for you.

3   _3rd_   _third_

7   _____   _____

8   _____   _____

10   _____   _____

Draw the number of items to match the position given.

2nd

_____

5th

_____

4th

_____

10th

_____

7th

OBJECTIVE: Use calendar, schedule to tell the position of an event.

Below are the days of the week. Answer the following questions.

Sunday	Monday	Tuesday	Wednesday	Thursday
1st	2nd	3rd	4th	5th
First	Second	Third	Fourth	Fifth

Friday	Saturday
6th	7th
Sixth	Seventh

1.   Which is the first day of the week? _____

2.   Which day is in the middle? _____

3.   Which is the last day of the week? _____

4.   Which is the third day of the week? _____

5.   Which is the sixth day of the week? _____

6.   Which is the first day of the school week? _____

7.   Which is the last day of the school week? _____

ORDINAL NUMBERS

Below is a part of a calendar. Use it to answer the following questions.

JULY 2017

Sunday	Monday	Tuesday	Wednesday	Thursday	Friday	Saturday
						1
2	3	4	5	6	7	8
9	10	11	12	13	14	15
16	17	18	19	20	21	22
23	24	25	26	27	28	29
30	31					

1. On what day did the month begin? _____

2. What is the twelfth day of this month? _____

3. On which day does the month end? _____

4. On which day is the first of August? _____

Circle true if the sentence is true or circle false if the sentence is false.

1. The sixteenth day of July is a Sunday.   True   False

2. This month has 3 Tuesdays.   True   False

3. This month has 5 Saturdays.   True   False

4. The day before the eighth day is a Thursday.   True   False

5. The day after the ninth day is a Monday.   True   False

6. The day before the sixth day is a Wednesday. True   False

JANUARY 2017 1st

Sun	Mon	Tue	Wed	Thu	Fri	Sat
1	2	3	4	5	6	7
8	9	10	11	12	13	14
15	16	17	18	19	20	21
22	23	24	25	26	27	28
29	30	31				

FEBRUARY 2017 2nd

Sun	Mon	Tue	Wed	Thu	Fri	Sat
			1	2	3	4
5	6	7	8	9	10	11
12	13	14	15	16	17	18
19	20	21	22	23	24	25
26	27	28				

MARCH 2017 3rd

Sun	Mon	Tue	Wed	Thu	Fri	Sat
			1	2	3	4
5	6	7	8	9	10	11
12	13	14	15	16	17	18
19	20	21	22	23	24	25
26	27	28	29	30	31	

APRIL 2017 4th

Sun	Mon	Tue	Wed	Thu	Fri	Sat
						1
2	3	4	5	6	7	8
9	10	11	12	13	14	15
16	17	18	19	20	21	22
23/30	24	25	26	27	28	29

MAY 2017 5th

Sun	Mon	Tue	Wed	Thu	Fri	Sat
	1	2	3	4	5	6
7	8	9	10	11	12	13
14	15	16	17	18	19	20
21	22	23	24	25	26	27
28	29	30	31			

JUNE 2017 6th

Sun	Mon	Tue	Wed	Thu	Fri	Sat
				1	2	3
4	5	6	7	8	9	10
11	12	13	14	15	16	17
18	19	20	21	22	23	24
25	26	27	28	29	30	31

JULY 2017 7th

Sun	Mon	Tue	Wed	Thu	Fri	Sat
						1
2	3	4	5	6	7	8
9	10	11	12	13	14	15
16	17	18	19	20	21	22
23	24	25	26	27	28	29
30	31					

AUGUST 2017 8th

Sun	Mon	Tue	Wed	Thu	Fri	Sat
		1	2	3	4	5
6	7	8	9	10	11	12
13	14	15	16	17	18	19
20	21	22	23	24	25	26
27	28	29	30	31		

SEPTEMBER 2017 9th

Sun	Mon	Tue	Wed	Thu	Fri	Sat
					1	2
3	4	5	6	7	8	9
10	11	12	13	14	15	16
17	18	19	20	21	22	23
24	25	26	27	28	29	30

OCTOBER 2017 10th

Sun	Mon	Tue	Wed	Thu	Fri	Sat
1	2	3	4	5	6	7
8	9	10	11	12	13	14
15	16	17	18	19	20	21
22	23	24	25	26	27	28
29	30	31				

NOVEMBER 2017 11th

Sun	Mon	Tue	Wed	Thu	Fri	Sat
			1	2	3	4
5	6	7	8	9	10	11
12	13	14	15	16	17	18
19	20	21	22	23	24	25
26	27	28	29	30	31	

DECEMBER 2017 12th

Sun	Mon	Tue	Wed	Thu	Fri	Sat
					1	2
3	4	5	6	7	8	9
10	11	12	13	14	15	16
17	18	19	20	21	22	23
24/31	25	26	27	28	29	30

Answer the following questions using the complete year's calendar above.

1. Which is the last month? _____

2. Which is the first month? _____

3. Which is the sixth month? _____

4. Which month is fourth? _____

15

ORDINAL NUMBERS

The Months of the year.

January is the first month - 1st

February is the second month - 2nd

March is the third month - 3rd

April is the fourth month - 4th

May is the fifth month - 5th

June is the sixth month - 6th

July is the seventh month - 7th

August is the eighth month - 8th

September is the ninth month - 9th

October is the tenth month - 10th

November is the eleventh month - 11th

December is the twelfth month - 12th

Answer these questions.

1. Which is the 6th month of the year? _____

2. Today is Monday, two days from now will be? _____

3. Tomorrow is Sunday, a day after will be? _____

4. Which is the 9th month of the year? _____

5. Today is Wednesday, tomorrow will be? _____

6. Yesterday was Saturday, tomorrow will be? _____

Complete this table.

Today is	Tomorrow will be	Yesterday was	Two days after yesterday will be	Two days ago it was
Monday				
Saturday				
Thursday				
Wednesday				
Friday				
Sunday				
Tuesday				

Read Jodi's daily schedule. (not including Saturday and Sunday)

TIME	ACTIVITIES
Morning 6:00 am to 7:30 am	Get out of bed. Pray Do bathroom duties. Brush teeth. Dress Eat breakfast. Off to school.
During the morning 8:00 am to 11:00 am	School work
11:05 – 11:45 11:45 – 12:00 12:00 – 2:00	Eat lunch. School activities School ends.
Afternoon to evening 3:00 pm to 7:00 pm	Return home from school. Eat snack. Do home chores. Do homework; study.
Night 7:00 pm to 9:00 pm	Help Mom with chores. Eat dinner. Watch television. Say prayers. Go to sleep.

Make up your own daily schedule.

My Daily Schedule

(not including Saturday and Sunday)

TIME	ACTIVITIES
Morning	
During the morning	
Afternoon	
Afternoon to evening	
Night	

ORDINAL NUMBERS

Match the Ordinal Numbers to their correct number names.

1st	fourth
2nd	ninth
3rd	fifth
4th	seventh
5th	eighth
6th	tenth
7th	third
8th	sixth
9th	first
10th	second

Answer the questions below.

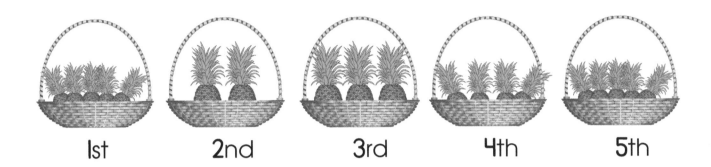

| 1st | 2nd | 3rd | 4th | 5th |

a. How many pineapples are there in the 4th basket?

_____

b. How many pineapples are there in the 3rd basket?

_____

c. How many pineapples are there in the fifth basket?

_____

d. How many pineapples are there in all, in both the 2nd and

the 3rd baskets? _____

e. What is the total number of pineapples in all the baskets?

_____

How many mangoes are there?

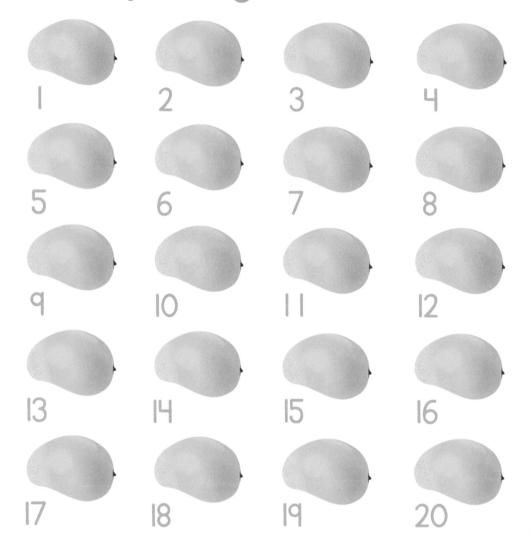

1   2   3   4

5   6   7   8

9   10   11   12

13   14   15   16

17   18   19   20

Look at the number line below.

Counting on the number line 1 - 20.

NUMBERS 10 TO 20

This is a number line from ten to twenty.

Study the numbers from ten to twenty.

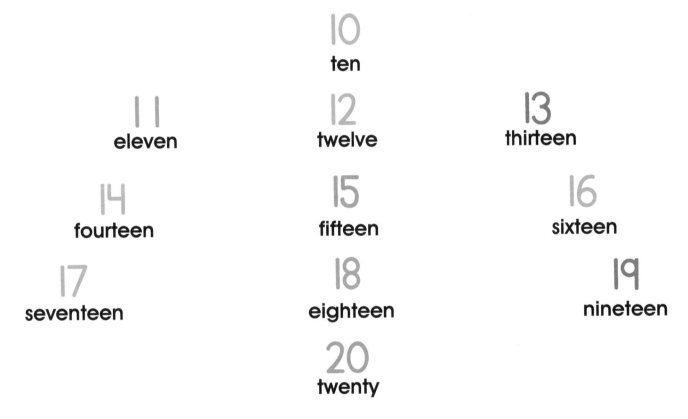

10
ten

11
eleven

12
twelve

13
thirteen

14
fourteen

15
fifteen

16
sixteen

17
seventeen

18
eighteen

19
nineteen

20
twenty

Count and colour the stars. How many are there? _____

NUMERALS AND THEIR NUMBER NAMES

Which numbers are not in the correct places?

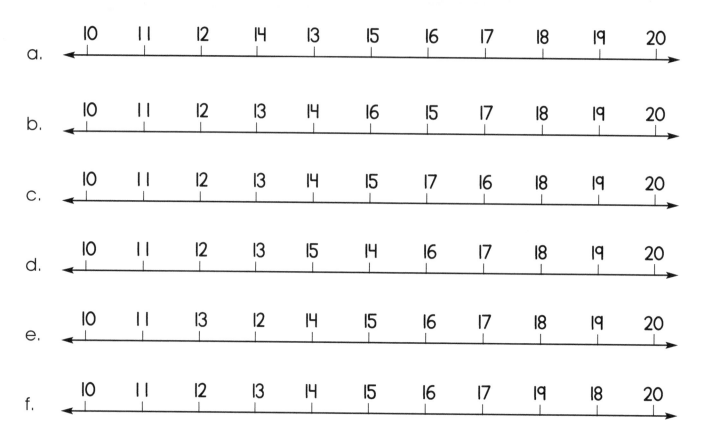

a.
b.
c.
d.
e.
f.

Count and colour the following shapes. How many shapes are there? Write the total in the box.

OBJECTIVE: Show the greatest or the least of a set of given numbers.

One more than and one greater than are the same. The number that is one greater than a given number comes after that given number.

Draw the number line from ten to twenty and use it to help you answer the questions if needed.

```
  10     11      12      14      13      15      16      17      18      19      20
 ←—┬——————┬——————┬——————┬——————┬——————┬——————┬——————┬——————┬——————┬——————┬——→
```

Answer the questions below.

a. What number is one more than sixteen? _____

b. What number comes after sixteen? _____

c. What number is one more than twelve? _____

d. What number comes after twelve? _____

e. What number is one more than fifteen? _____

Answer the questions below.

a. What number is one less than eleven? _____

b. What number comes before eleven? _____

c. What number is one less than thirteen? _____

d. What number comes before thirteen? _____

e. What number is one less than eighteen? _____

OBJECTIVE: Associate numerals with words.

Draw objects to show the number below each shape. The first one is done for you.

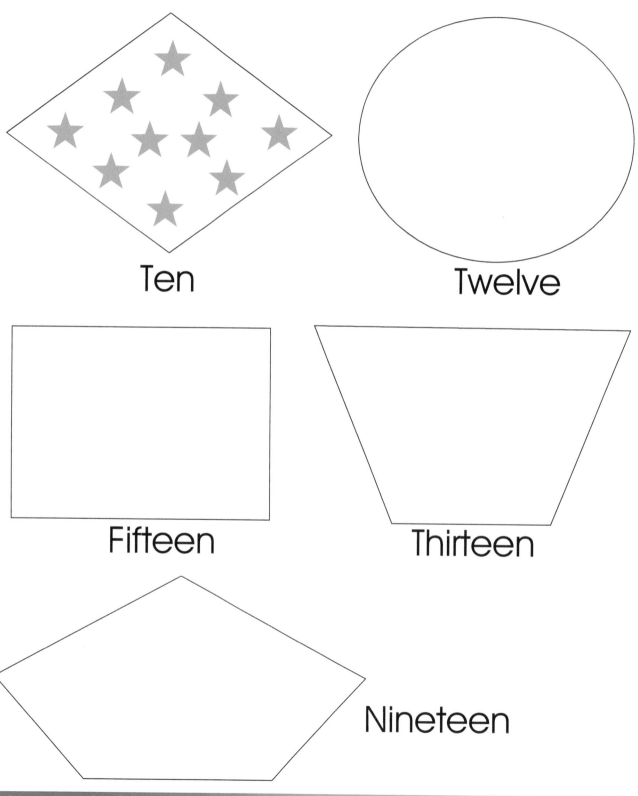

Ten

Twelve

Fifteen

Thirteen

Nineteen

What is One More?

7

8

1 more than 7 is 8.

Redraw and add 1 more to each set.

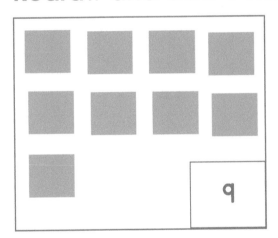

q

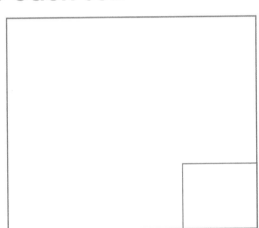

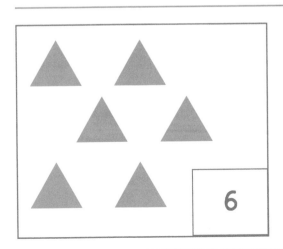

6

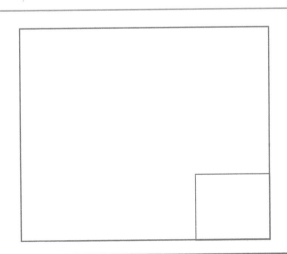

Redraw and add 1 more to each set.

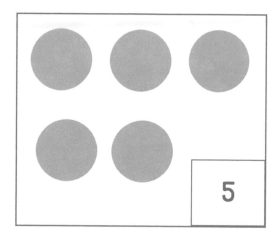

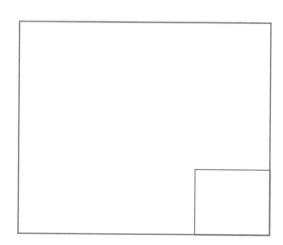

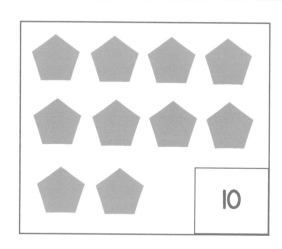

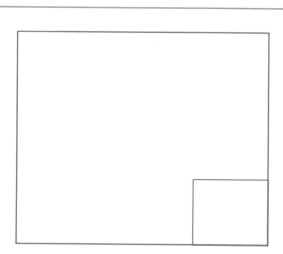

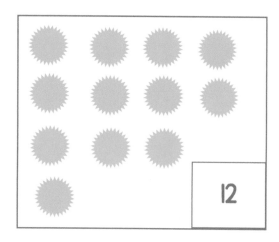

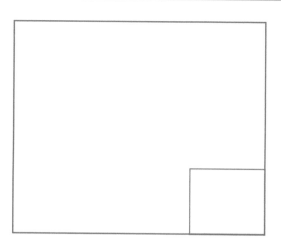

Write the numerals that correspond to the names below.

Twelve _____   Twenty _____   Thirteen _____

Fourteen _____   Eighteen _____   Seventeen _____

1. Circle the group with ten kites.

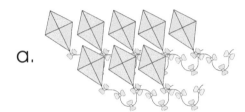   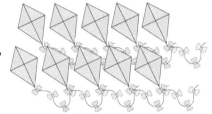   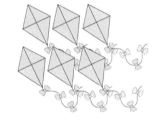

a.   b.   c.

2. Circle the group with twelve turtles.

a.   b   c.

3. Circle the group with fifteen oranges.

a.   b.   c.

4. Circle the group with eleven bananas.

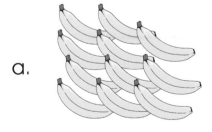   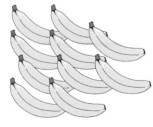   

a.   b.   c.

OBJECTIVE: Identify the next number in any sequence of counting numbers.

The number line can be used to show the order in which numbers appear. You have learnt that one comes after zero while five comes before six.

Answer the following questions.

a. Which number comes after nineteen? _____

b. Which number comes after sixteen? _____

c. Which number comes after eleven? _____

d. Which number comes after fifteen? _____

e. Which number comes after ten? _____

Answer the following questions by stating **TRUE** or **FALSE**.

Ten comes after nineteen? _____

Twenty comes after the number eleven? _____

Fourteen comes before fifteen? _____

Seventeen comes before sixteen? _____

Twelve comes after ten? _____

How many carrots are there?

How many pineapples are there?

Put each of the following sets of numbers in order from the least to the greatest. Use a number line to help you, if needed.

a.   10,   12,   15,   11,   13   19,   14,   18,   16,   17

____, ____, ____, ____, ____, ____, ____, ____, ____, ____

b.   twelve,   fourteen,   thirteen,   fifteen,   eleven

_____, _____, _____, _____, _____

c.   Twenty,   19,   Fifteen,   16,   Eighteen,   Seventeen

_____, _____, _____, _____, _____, _____

d.   11,   12,   Ten,   15,   13,   Fourteen

_____, _____, _____, _____, _____, _____

Fill in the missing numerals.

Write how many cows there are _____.

a.
		15			19	

b.
10				14			

c.
13			16				

d.
11						18

NUMERALS AND THEIR NUMBER NAMES

This is part of a calendar. Use it to answer the questions that follow.

Sunday	Monday	Tuseday	Wednesday	Thursday	Friday	Saturday
	1	2	3	4	5	6
7	8	9	10		12	13
14	15		17	18	19	
21	22	23	24	25	26	27
28	29	30	31			

KEY

Sunny

Cloud Cover
(but no Rain)

Rain

Windy

a. From the calendar above which numbers are missing? _____

b. Which three days have rain? Write the numerals in words. _____

_____

_____

c. Which days have cloud cover but no rain? Write the numerals in words. _____

_____

d. Which days are sunny? _____

_____

Colour the numerals and match them to their correct names. The first one is done for you.

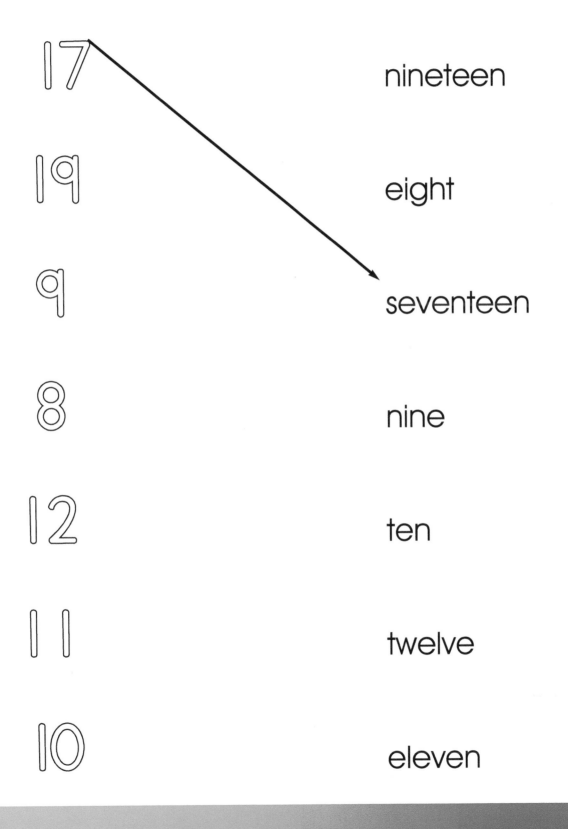

17

19

9

8

12

11

10

nineteen

eight

seventeen

nine

ten

twelve

eleven

Write the correct numeral beside each number name.

eight		nineteen
eleven		six
three		seventeen
nine		twenty
eighteen		two
four		one
ten		sixteen
five		seven
twelve		fourteen
thirteen		fifteen

Trace the numerals from 1 to 20.

1	2	3	4	5
6	7	8	9	10
11	12	13	14	15
16	17	18	19	20

Write the correct numerals.

1	2		4		6		8		10
11									20

Write the correct numerals.

3, 4, 5   2, 3, 4   5, 6, 7

1, 2, __   __, 19, 20   6, 7, __

15, 16, __   __, 9, 10   17, 18, __

11, 12, __   __, 5, 6   16, 17, __

Connect the dots in order. Begin with 1.

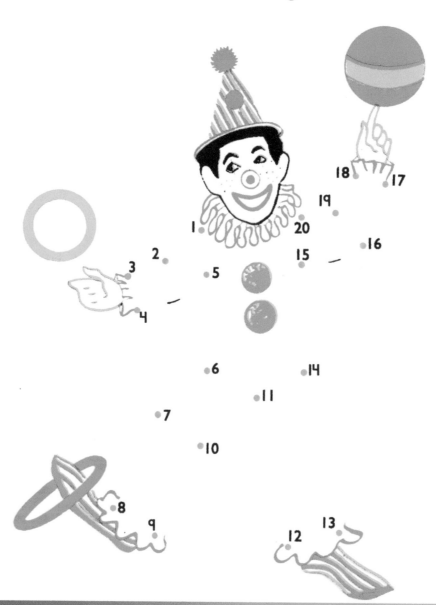

How Many?

When we put sets of things together, we are adding.

We use the addition sign + plus which tells us that we must add.

This sign = means equal.

Example:

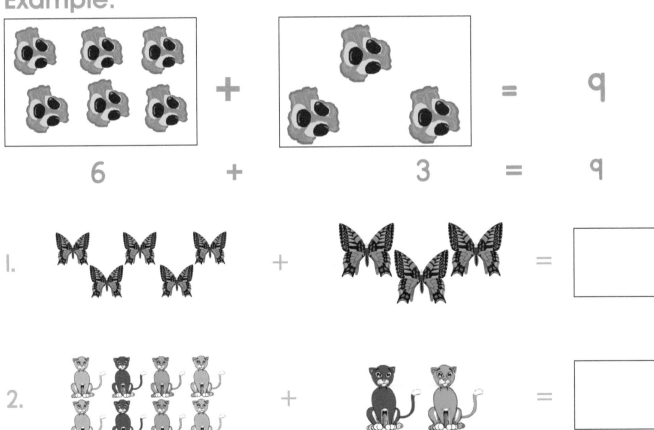

6   +   3   =   9

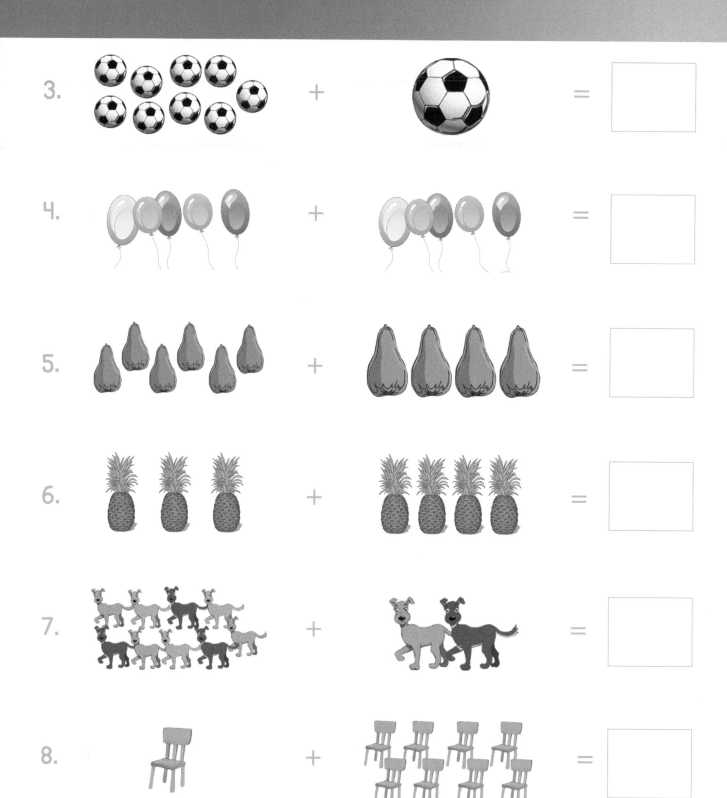

3.

4.

5.

6.

7.

8.

OBJECTIVE: Explain the meaning of zero in addition.

When we add 0 to a set we get the same number.

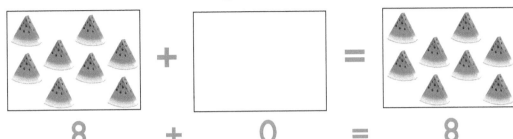

Example: 8   +   0   =   8

Now do these.

1.   0   +   5   =   [ ]

4.   12   +   0   =   [ ]

2.   10   +   0   =   [ ]

5.   9   +   0   =   [ ]

3.   3   +   0   =   [ ]

Finish these.

5 birds   +   5 birds   =   [ ]

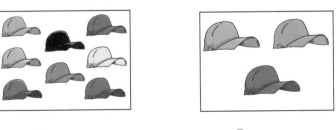

8 caps   +   3 caps   =   [ ]

HOW MANY?

 10 cats +  2 cats =

 7 dogs +  2 dogs =

1. 5 + 3 = ☐

2. 2 + 3 = ☐

3. 4 + 6 = ☐

4. 5 + 5 = ☐

5. 4 + 3 = ☐

6. 6 + 5 = ☐

7. 7 + ☐ = 9

8. 2 + ☐ = 6

9. 9 + 0 = ☐

10. 3 + 6 = ☐

11. 7 + 2 = ☐

12. 2 + 2 = ☐

13. 5 + 2 = ☐

14. 6 + 1 = ☐

15. 4 + ☐ = 8

16. 4 + 4 = ☐

17. 0 + ☐ = 8

18. 7 + 1 = ☐

Sets

What is a set?

A number of things or people grouped together is called a set.

Match the sets with their numerals. One is done for you.

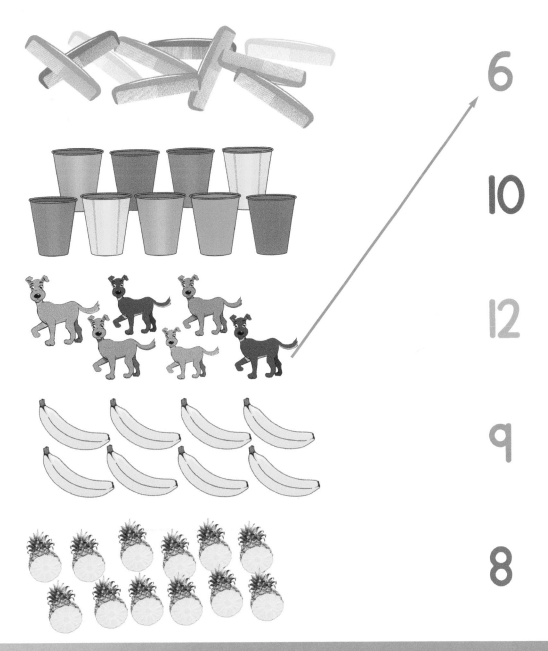

6

10

12

q

8

OBJECTIVE: Identify by counting the numer of members in a set.

Can you write the number name for each one of these sets?

How many members are there in each set?
Circle the correct numeral.

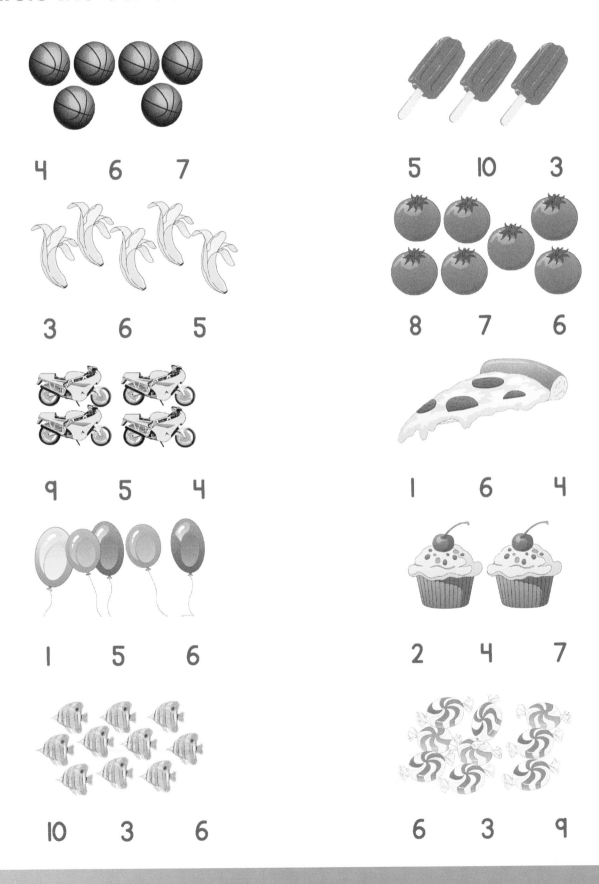

4   6   7

5   10   3

3   6   5

8   7   6

9   5   4

1   6   4

1   5   6

2   4   7

10   3   6

6   3   9

How many?

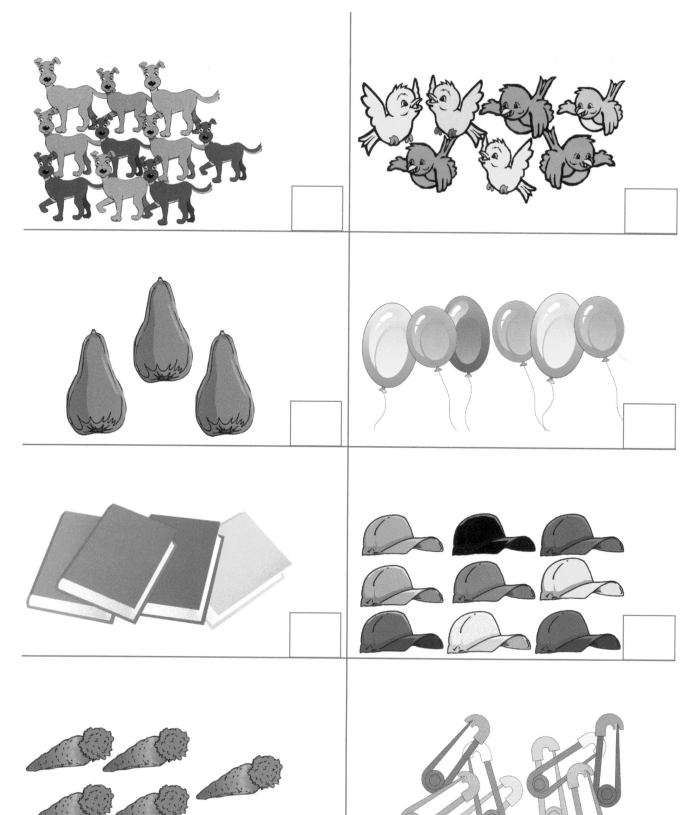

Match the numeral with the correct set.

12

10

8

9

7

6

4

5

Circle the sets of 7.

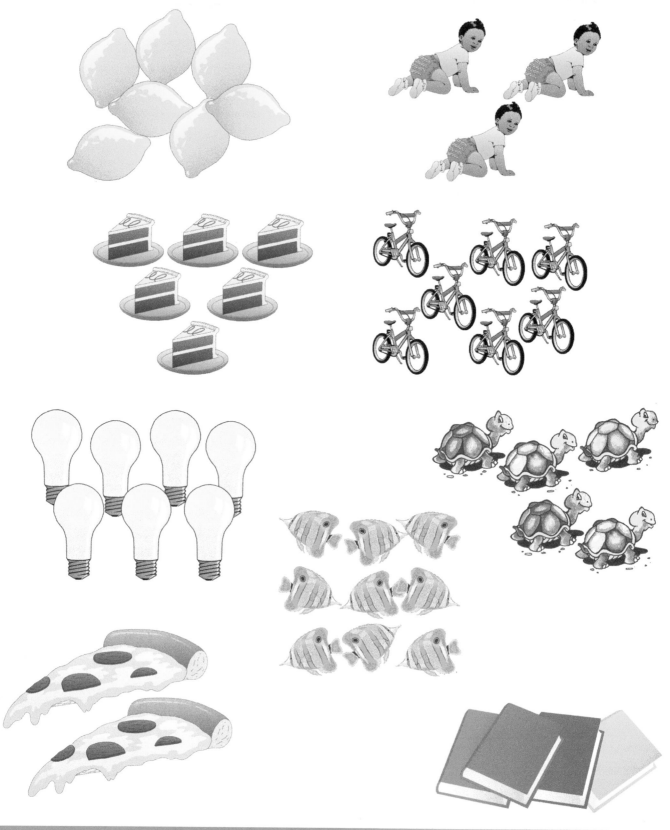

Circle the correct numeral in each set.

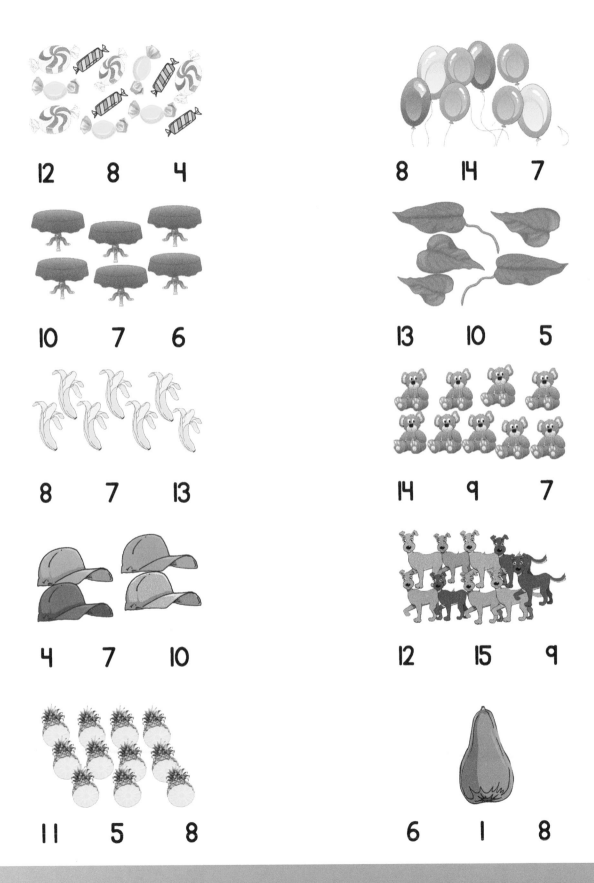

12   8   4

8   14   7

10   7   6

13   10   5

8   7   13

14   9   7

4   7   10

12   15   9

11   5   8

6   1   8

Circle the sets of 9.

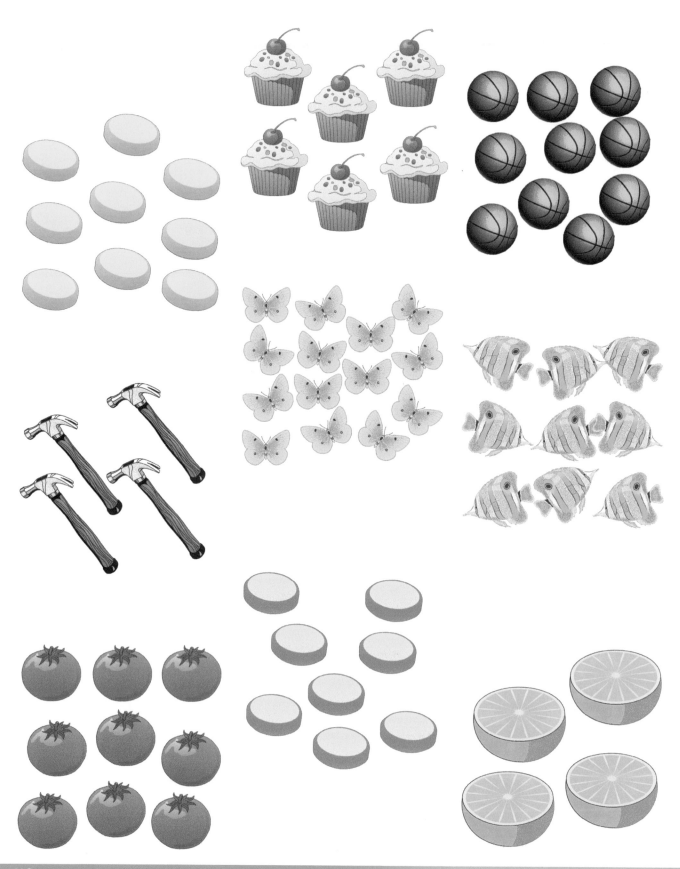

Draw sets for these numerals.

7

9

6

4

5

10

What is an empty set?

This is an empty set.
An empty set is a set
that has nothing in it.

Can you finish each sentence?

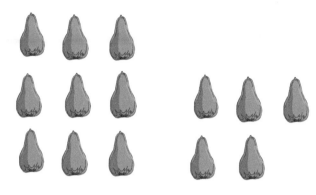

2 apples + 6 apples = [ ]

9 apples + 5 apples = [ ]

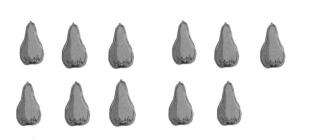

6 apples + 5 apples = [ ]

11 apples + 2 apples = [ ]

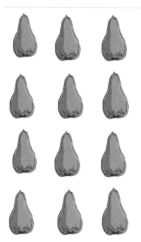

12 apples + 0 apples = [ ]

9 apples + 0 apples = [ ]

10 birds + 5 birds =

6 birds + 0 birds =

5 birds + 7 birds =

9 birds + 0 birds =

15 birds + 2 birds =

7 birds + 5 birds =

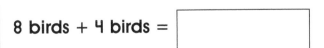

10 birds + 0 birds =

8 birds + 4 birds =

Tell how many items there are in each set. Write in the number name as well as the numeral. The first one is done for you.

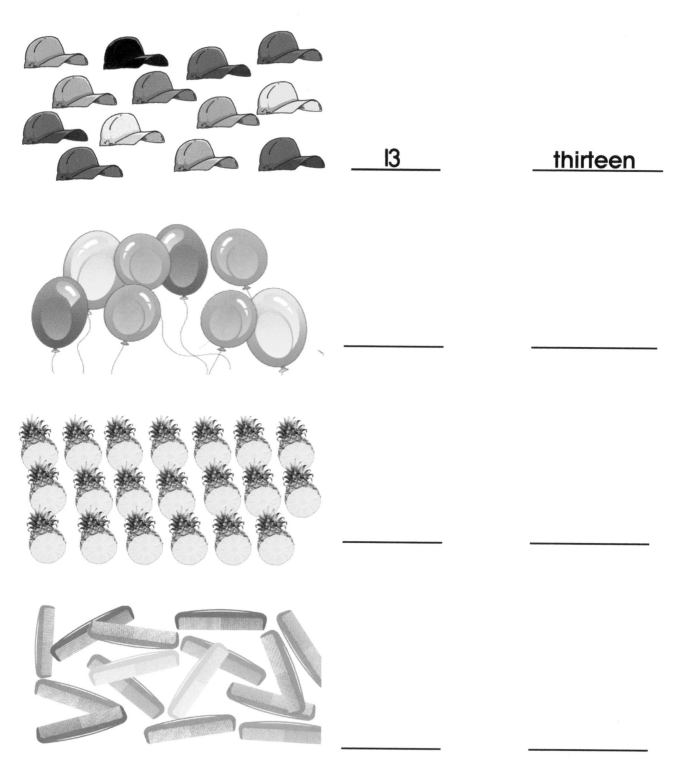

___13___   ___thirteen___

_____   _____

_____   _____

_____   _____

Comparing

Is Equal To

Set A

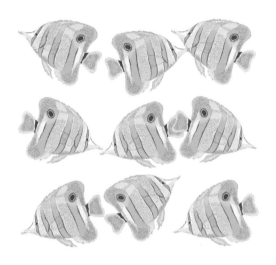

Set B

Count the number of members in Set A. Now count the number of members in Set B.

1. Set A has _____ members. Set B has _____ members.

2. Set _____ is equal to Set _____.

Mark the sets that are equal in the row.

Make the Set B equal to Set A, by drawing the missing members.

Set A 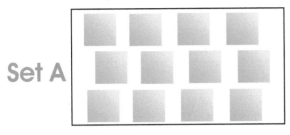   Set B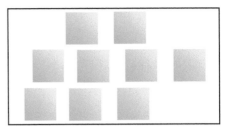

Set A is equal to Set B.

Set A 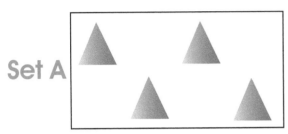   Set B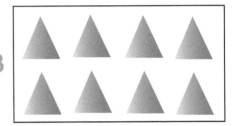

Set A is equal to Set B.

Set A 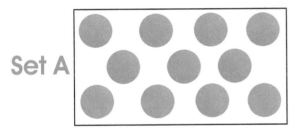   Set B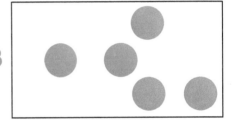

Set A is equal to Set B.

Set A    Set B

Set A is equal to Set B.

Set A    Set B

Set A is equal to Set B.

IS EQUAL TO/THE SAME

This symbol = means equal to, or the same.

 =    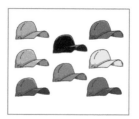 =

 =     =

Put a numeral in each circle to make the sentence true.

1. **7** =   6. **3** =

2. **6** = ◯   7. **4** = ◯

3. **8** = ◯   8. **10** =

4. **9** = ◯   9. **1** =

5. **5** = ◯   10. **2** =

Before and After

1. The number before 10 is ☐

2. The number after 10 is ☐

3. The number after 12 is ☐

4. The number before 6 is ☐

5. The number after 19 is ☐

6. The number before 15 is ☐

7. The number after 17 is ☐

8. The number before 20 is ☐

9. The number after 18 is ☐

10. The number after 11 is ☐

11. The number before 18 is ☐

12. The number before 13 is ☐

Is Greater Than

Sets that have more members than others are said to be greater than.

Examples:

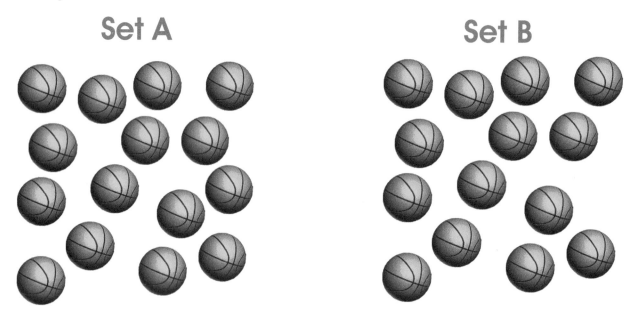

Set A   Set B

Count the number of members in Set A. Now count the number of members in Set B. Which set has more members?

1. Set _____ has more members than Set _____

2. Set _____ is greater than Set _____.

Let us look at another example.

Set A

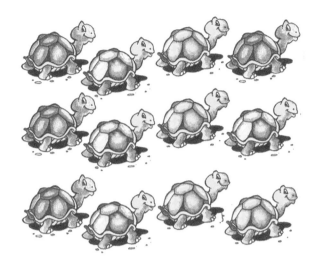

Set B

1. Set A has _____ members. Set B has _____ members.

2. Set _____ has more members than Set _____.

3. Set _____ is greater than Set _____.

Count and circle. Which Set is greater?

Set A

Set B

Look at Set A and Set B. Fill in the blank spaces.

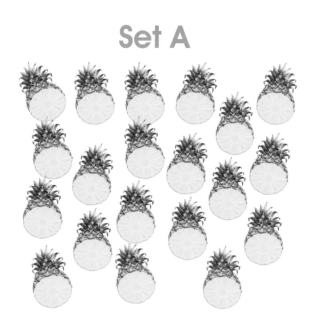

1. There are _____ pineapples in Set A and _____ pineapples in Set B.

2. Which set has more pineapples? _____.

3. Set _____ has more pineapples than Set _____.

4. Set _____ is greater than Set _____.

Set A

Set B

1. There are _____ cats in Set A and _____ cats in Set B.

2. Which set has more cats?

3. Set _____ has more cats than Set _____.

4. Set _____ is greater than Set _____.

Set A

Set B

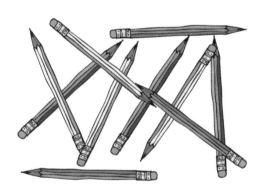

1. There are _____ pencils in Set A and _____ pencils in Set B.

2. Which set has more pencils?

3. Set _____ has more pencils than Set _____.

Circle the set that is greater.

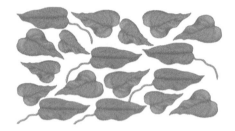 

Circle the set that is greater.

Is Less Than

Some sets have less members than others. These are said to be **Less than.**

Example:

Set A   Set B

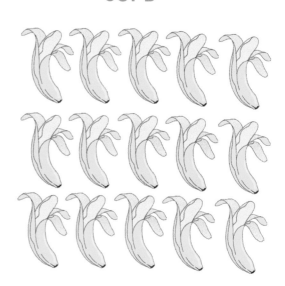

1. Count the number of members in Set A. _____

2. Now count the number of members in Set B. _____

3. Which set has less members? _____

4. Set _____ has less members than Set _____.

5. Set _____ is less than Set _____.

Activity:

Let us look at another example.

Set A

Set B

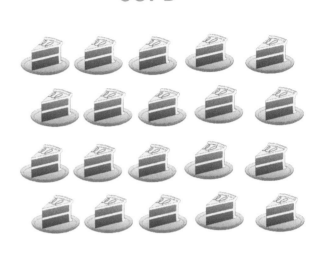

1. Set A has _____ members. Set B has _____ members.

2. Set _____ has less members than Set _____.

3. Set _____ is less than Set _____.

Count and circle. Which Set is less?

Set A

Set B

Write either T for True or F for False in the blank space.

1. 4 is less than 8. _____

2. 10 is greater than 7. _____

3. 8 is grearter than 6. _____

4. 14 is less than 15. _____

5. 19 is less than 20. _____

6. 11 is greater than 9. _____

7. 15 is less than 17. _____

OBJECTIVE: Use the following symbols when comparing >, <, =.

We can use the symbol for greater than ">" which points to the right and the symbol for less than "<" which points to the left.

Use these symbols > or < or the equal sign = to make each sentence true.

1. 9 ☐ 9

2. 4 ☐ 10

3. 6 ☐ 8

4. 5 ☐ 5

5. 2 ☐ 2

6. 10 ☐ 9

7. 3 ☐ 0

8. 6 ☐ 3

We can use the symbol for greater than ">" which points to the right and the symbol for less than "<" which points to the left.

Put the numerals for each set in the boxes. Put in > or < to make the statement true. The first one is done for you.

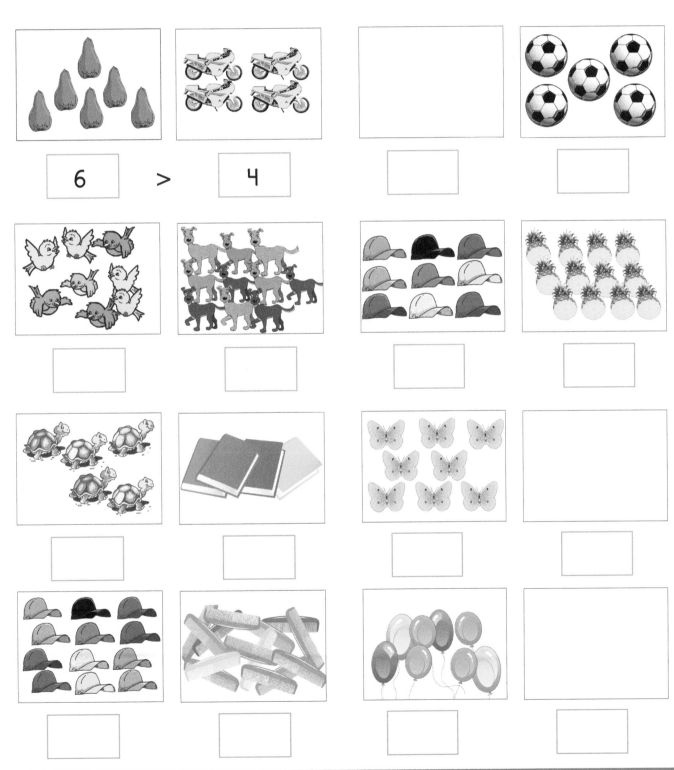

Make the sentences true by drawing members in each section.

> ■■■ ■■■	●●●● ●●● ●● >
●●●● ●●● ●●● >	> ★★ ★★★
★★★ ★★★ >	⬠⬠⬠ >
⬠⬠⬠ ⬠⬠⬠ >	▬▬▬ ▬▬▬ ▬▬ >

Put a numeral in each empty box to make the sentence true.

1. [7] > [4]   7. [4] > [   ]

2. [   ] > [5]   8. [7] > [   ]

3. [8] > [   ]   9. [   ] > [7]

4. [10] > [   ]   10. [   ] > [5]

5. [   ] > [6]   11. [8] > [   ]

6. [9] > [   ]   12. [5] > [   ]

IS EQUAL TO/THE SAME

This symbol = means equal to, or the same.

 =  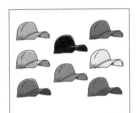 =

 =   =

Put a numeral in each circle to make the sentence true.

1. 7 = ◯   6. 3 = ◯

2. 6 = ◯   7. 4 = ◯

3. 8 = ◯   8. 10 = ◯

4. 9 = ◯   9. 1 = ◯

5. 5 = ◯   10. 2 = ◯

Before and After

1. The number before 11 is ⬜

2. The number after 12 is ⬜

3. The number after 14 is ⬜

4. The number before 9 is ⬜

5. The number after 18 is ⬜

6. The number before 16 is ⬜

7. The number after 13 is ⬜

8. The number before 21 is ⬜

9. The number after 15 is ⬜

10. The number after 10 is ⬜

11. The number before 17 is ⬜

12. The number before 12 is ⬜

Measurement

LET US READ

Metres and Centimetres

1 metre = 100 centimetres

1 m = 100 cm

The metre is used to measure long distances. Roadways, buildings and playing fields are some examples when the metre is used. For smaller objects we measure lengths using the centimetre. Use paper clips to measure the lengths of the following:

We use m for metre and cm for centimetre

The length of the pencil is _____ paper clips long.

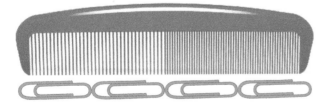

The length of the comb is_____ paper clips long.

The length of the exercise book is _____ paper clips long.

71

MEASUREMENT

ESTIMATE LENGTHS (QUANTITY)

How long?

Find the following items in your classroom. Use the paper clips to measure their lengths.

A pencil

Guess:_____ paper clips long

Measure: _____ paper clips long

An exercise book

Guess:_____ paper clips long

Measure: _____ paper clips long

A mathematics book

Guess:_____ paper clips long

Measure: _____ paper clips long

A lunch kit

Guess:_____ paper clips long

Measure: _____ paper clips long

OBJECTIVE: Use ruler carefully to measure.

Use a centimetre ruler to measure the lengths of the following:

Look at a centimetre ruler. It is marked in centimetres, cm.

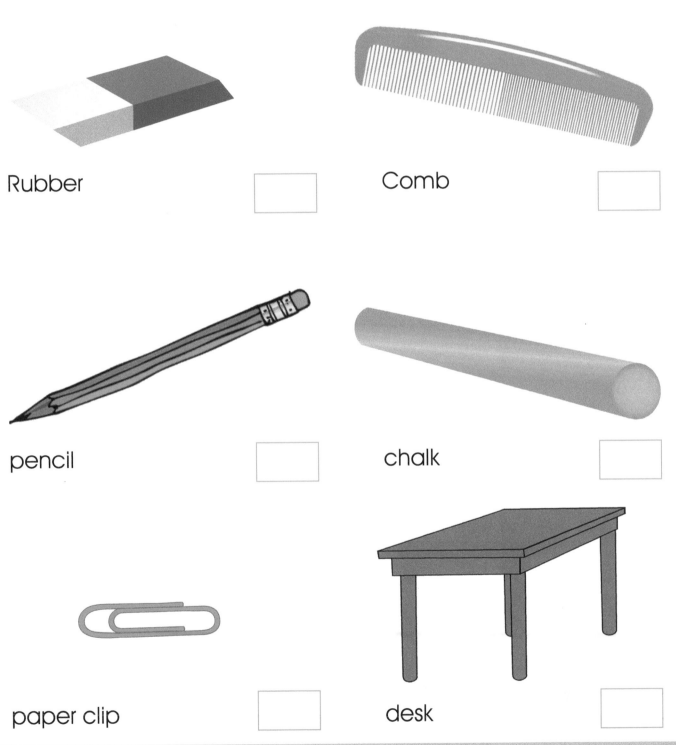

Rubber

Comb

pencil

chalk

paper clip

desk

MEASUREMENT: METRES AND CENTIMETRES

Measure the length of the lines. Put each measurement in the correct box.

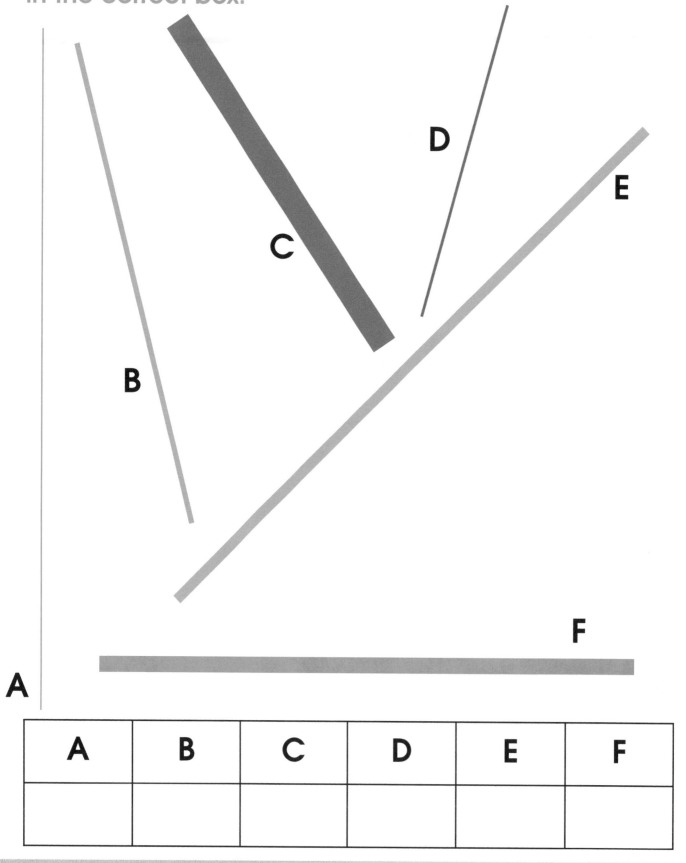

A	B	C	D	E	F

Measure the lengths around the figures with a thread. Mark the long sides with a ✓. Mark the short sides with an X.

MEASUREMENT: METRES AND CENTIMETRES

The best way to measure length is with a ruler.

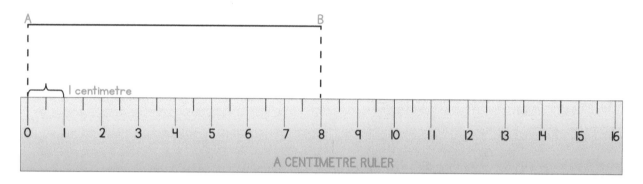

This is a picture of a centimetre ruler.

The length of each big division is 1 centimetre.

The length of line AB is **8** centimetres.

8 centimetres can also be written as **8** cm.

Use the centimetre ruler to measure the length of this piece of chalk.

The piece of chalk is _____ cm long.

Use your ruler to measure the following:

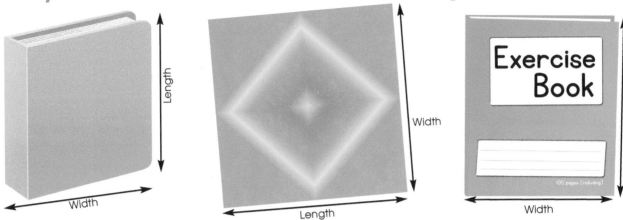

Length of the exercise book	_____ cm
Width of the exercise book	_____ cm
Length of the book	_____ cm
Width of the book	_____ cm
Length of the coloured gift box	_____ cm
Width of the coloured gift box	_____ cm

How long are the sides of these shapes?

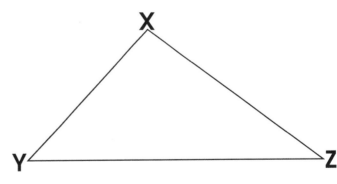

AB = _____ cm   XY = _____ cm

AD = _____ cm   YZ = _____ cm

BC = _____ cm   XZ = _____ cm

Use your cm ruler to find the lengths of the following objects.

1. Length of the teacher's desk top

    _____ cm

2. Length of the duster (eraser) in class

    _____ cm

3. Length of the classroom floor

    _____ cm

4. Length of a pencil _____ cm

5. Length of an exercise book

    _____ cm

6. Length of the chalkboard

    _____ cm

7. Length of one wall in the class

    _____ cm

MEASUREMENT: METRES AND CENTIMETRES

Cut a piece of cord 1 metre in length to measure the following objects. Before measuring guess their measurements, then measure to see how accurate you were.

Guess: The length of the chalkboard is about _____ metres.

Correct Measurement: _____ metres.

Guess: The height of the classroom door is about _____ metres.

Correct Measurement: _____ metres.

Guess: The height of your classmate is about _____ metres.

Correct Measurement: _____ metres.

Guess: The length of the classroom is about _____ metres.

Correct Measurement: _____ metres.

Guess: The width of the classroom is about _____ metres.

Correct Measurement: _____ metres.

Draw lines of these lengths.

5 cm

7 cm

10 cm

12 cm

Measure these lines in cm. Write the lengths beside or below the lines.

_____cm

_____cm

_____cm

_____cm

_____cm

I Can Count

NUMERALS AND
THEIR NUMBER NAMES: 20 - 30

Count the members in each set and write the correct numeral in the box for each set.

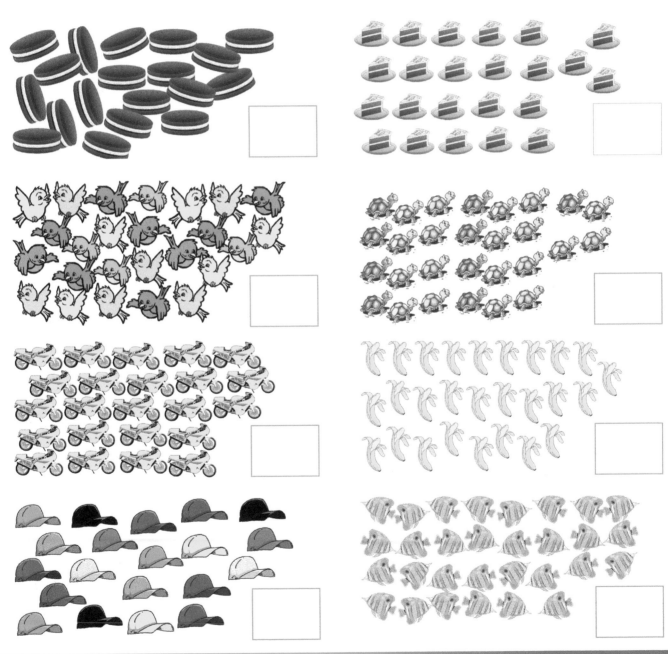

Match number names to their numerals.

23	**thirty**
27	twenty-six
29	twenty-one
25	twenty
18	twenty-seven
20	**twenty-five**
30	twenty-three
26	**twenty-nine**
21	eighteen

Trace the numerals from 20 to 30.

20	21	22	23	24	25
26	27	28	29	30	

Fill in the missing numerals.

1		3		5
	7		9	
11			14	
	17			20
		23		
		28		30

Draw objects in the spaces to match the numerals.

20	o o o o o o o o o o o o o o o o o o o o	twenty
21		twenty-one
22		twenty-two
23		twenty-three
24		twenty-four
25		twenty-five

26		twenty-six
27		twenty-seven
28		twenty-eight
29		twenty-nine
30		thirty

Find the correct number name for each.

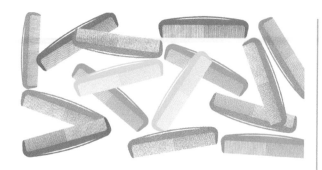

a. twelve   b. fifteen

c. fourteen

a. thirty   b. twenty-one

c. twenty-eight

a. eleven   b. twenty-nine

c. twenty-one

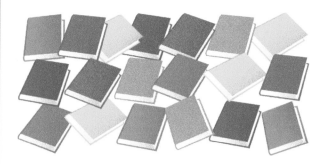

a. nineteen b. sixteen

c. twenty-three

a. fifteen   b. twenty-seven

c. nineteen

a. twenty-two   b. thirteen

c. twenty-four

Measurement

WEIGHING THINGS

When we want to know how much a thing weighs, we use a scale. There are many kinds of scales. Here are a few.

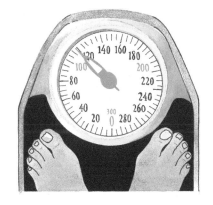

This is the scale used in the bathroom. We use it to weigh ourselves.

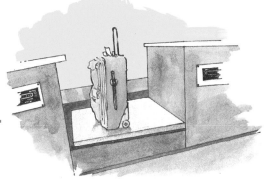

This scale is used at the airport for weighing the luggage of travellers.

This scale is found in many homes. It is used for measuring food items.

This scale is used by vendors who sell food products especially at the markets.

We weigh things in kilograms.

Each of these can be weighed in kilograms.

OBJECTIVE: Estimate the weight of given objects.

Which one weighs more? X those that you think weigh more.

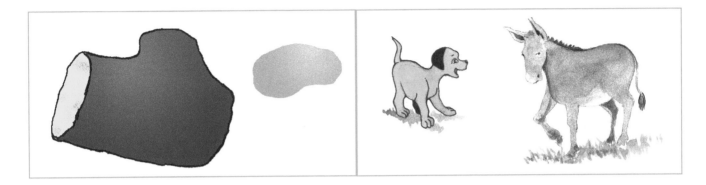

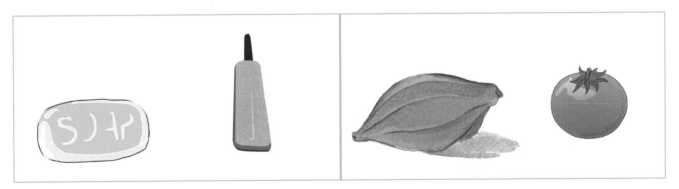

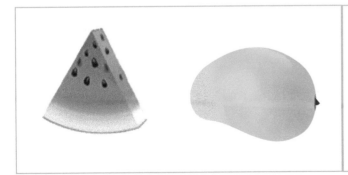 

Let us do an activity.

Place a pencil in the palm of your left hand. Now place an exercise book in the palm of your right hand. Which object feels heavier? Which is lighter?

_____ heavier　　_____ lighter

The Balance

A balance is used to show us if an object is heavy or light.

When one side of the balance is lower than the other because of the size of the object in it, we say that the lower side is heavier. The higher side is lighter.

OBJECTIVE: Use the balance scale to compare weight.

Let us compare.

Which side is heavier?

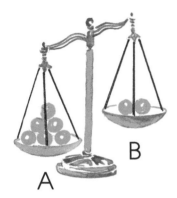

We can say side _____ is heavier than side _____.

We can say side _____ is lighter than side _____.

The balance is said to be even or equal when no side is heavier or lighter than the other. We say, they are the same.

Mass

Who is heavier/lighter? _____

Which is heavier/lighter? _____

Finding Mass in Units

Use marbles and a balance to find the masses of a small ball, an orange, a pencil, a handkerchief, a crayon and an eraser.

I stands for I unit.   **Example:**

Do these:

I stands for I unit.

a) What is the mass of the mango?   [   ] units

b) What is the mass of the eraser?   [   ] units

c) What is the mass of the book?   [   ] units

d) Which object is the heaviest?   [   ] units

e) Which is the lightest object?   [   ] units

Fill in the blanks. Use 🫘 as 1 unit.

a) The mass of carrots is _____ units.

b) The mass of the pineapple is _____ units.

c) The mass of the watermelon is _____ units.

Fill in the blanks. Use 🫘 as 1 unit.

a) The mass of the papaya is _____ units.

b) The mass of 2 papayas is _____ units.

a) The mass of the pineapple is _____ units.

b) The pineapple is as heavy as _____ units.

Using a scale

Let your teacher show you how to use and read the bathroom scale. Weigh yourself and then have three of your classmates weigh themselves. Write down the weights.

_____kg

Put your name in the box.

_____kg

Name of classmate 1

_____kg

Name of classmate 2

_____kg

Name of classmate 3

Who weighs the most? _____

Let us compare weights

We can compare weights by using the symbols

>   more than,   <   less than, or

=   equal (the same)

Compare the following using the symbols. >, < or =

1.   9 kg   ☐   12 kg   6.   10 kg   ☐   10 kg

2.   3 kg   ☐   3 kg   7.   5 kg   ☐   9 kg

3.   6 kg   ☐   5 kg   8.   11 kg   ☐   9 kg

4.   8 kg   ☐   14 kg   9.   11 kg   ☐   7 kg

5.   7 kg   ☐   7 kg   10.   15 kg   ☐   12 kg

Weight

ACTIVITY: COMPARISON OF WEIGHT

1. Put a papaya on one measuring pan, and an apple on the other measuring pan. Which one is heavier?

2. Add more apples to the measuring pan until the two pans balance.

Which is heavier? Circle it.

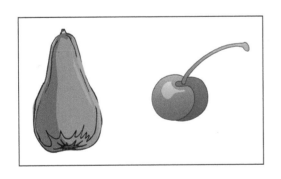

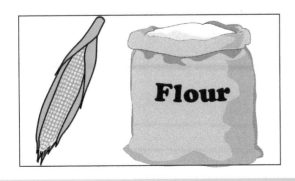

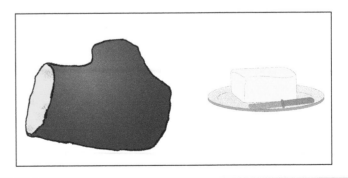

Which is lighter? Circle A or B

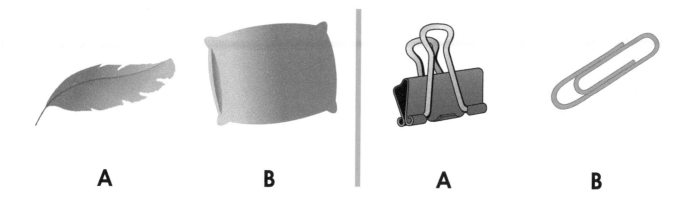

| A | B | A | B |

Look around your classroom and circle the items which are lighter.

1.   chair / desk   2.   pencil / eraser

3.   chalk / duster   4.   teacher / classmate

5.   textbook / notebook   6.   glue stick / ruler

7.   school bag / lunch bag   8.   box of crayons / tape

Which is heavier? Circle A or B

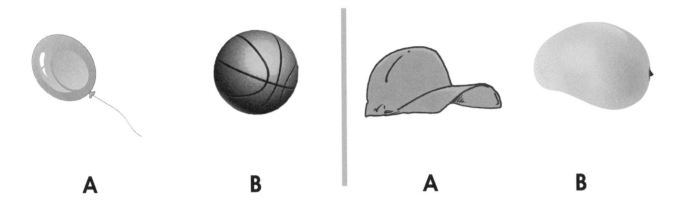

| A | B | A | B |

Look around your classroom and circle the items which are heavier.

1. teacher / classmate

2. textbook / notebook

3. box of crayons / tape

4. desk / chair

5. eraser / pencil

6. school bag / lunch bag

7. glue stick / ruler

8. duster / chalk

THE CLOCK

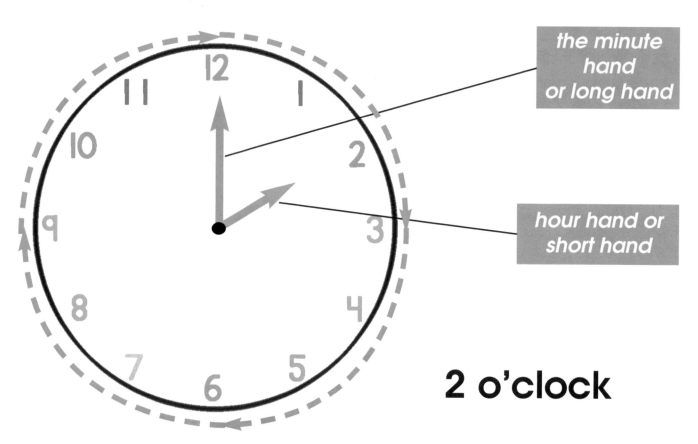

the minute hand or long hand

hour hand or short hand

2 o'clock

The long hand is the minute hand. It tells the minutes.

The short hand is the hour hand. It tells the hours.

All clocks or watches have the two hands. Some clocks and watches have a third hand which is the second hand. This hand tells the seconds.

OBJECTIVE: Tell the time (read the clock) on the hour and half hour.

When the long hand is on 12 and the short hand is on a number, that number tellls the hour. We write four o'clock like this: 4 o'clock or 4:00.

Examples:

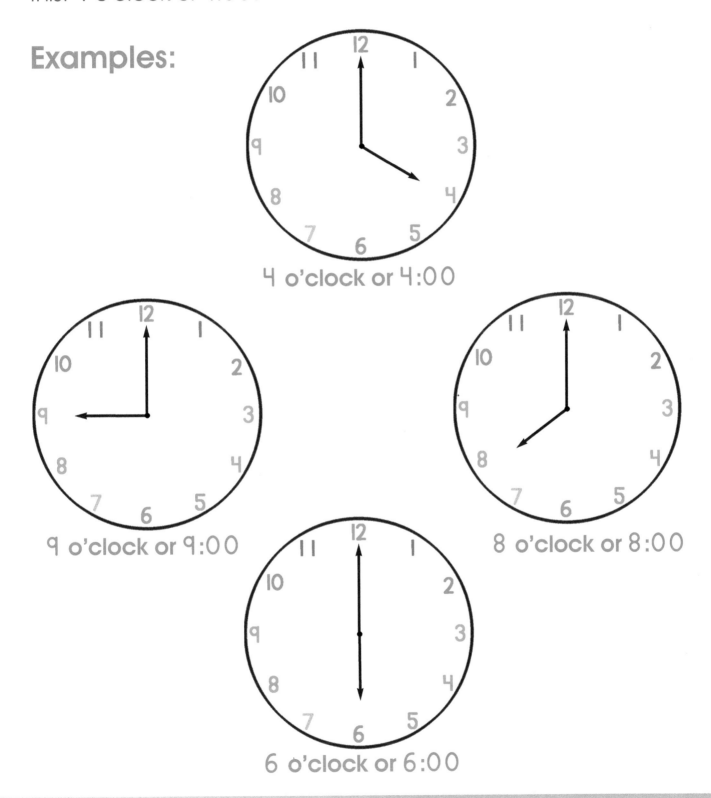

4 o'clock or 4:00

9 o'clock or 9:00

8 o'clock or 8:00

6 o'clock or 6:00

What time is it? Telling the time

It is 7 o'clock

It is _____ o'clock

It is _____ o'clock

It is _____ o'clock

It is _____ o'clock

It is _____ o'clock

It is _____ o'clock

It is _____ o'clock

Draw the correct time.

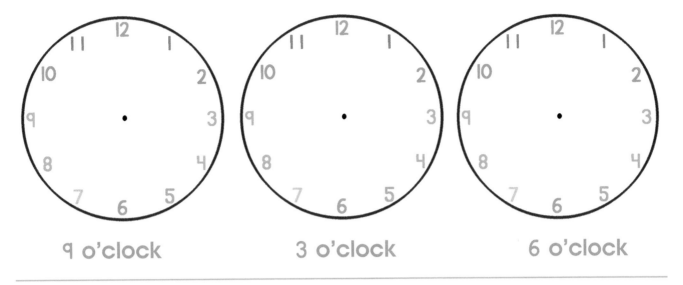

9 o'clock   3 o'clock   6 o'clock

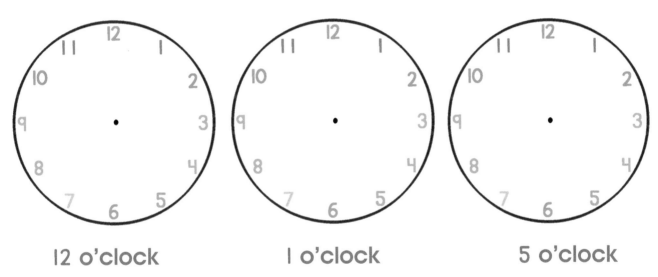

12 o'clock   1 o'clock   5 o'clock

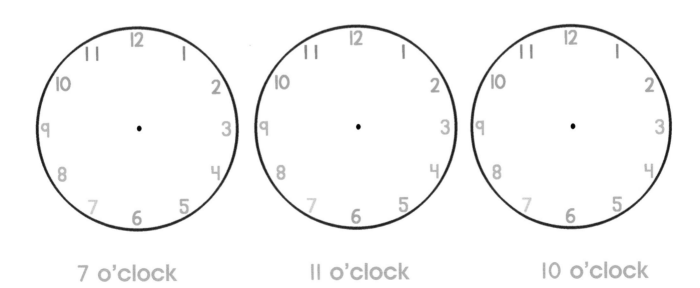

7 o'clock   11 o'clock   10 o'clock

What time is it?

Remember when the long hand (minute hand) points to 12 and the short hand (hour hand) points to any number on the clock face, the time is that hour.

Write the times shown on these clocks.

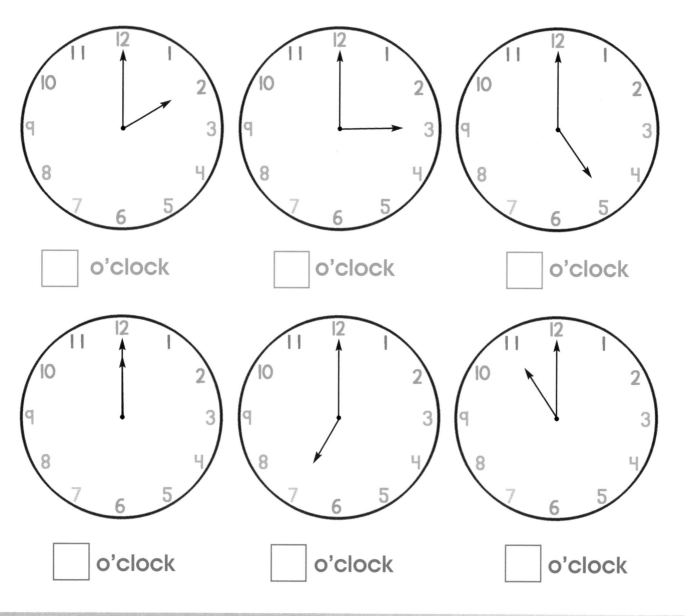

☐ o'clock   ☐ o'clock   ☐ o'clock

☐ o'clock   ☐ o'clock   ☐ o'clock

Which clock shows the correct time? Mark it!

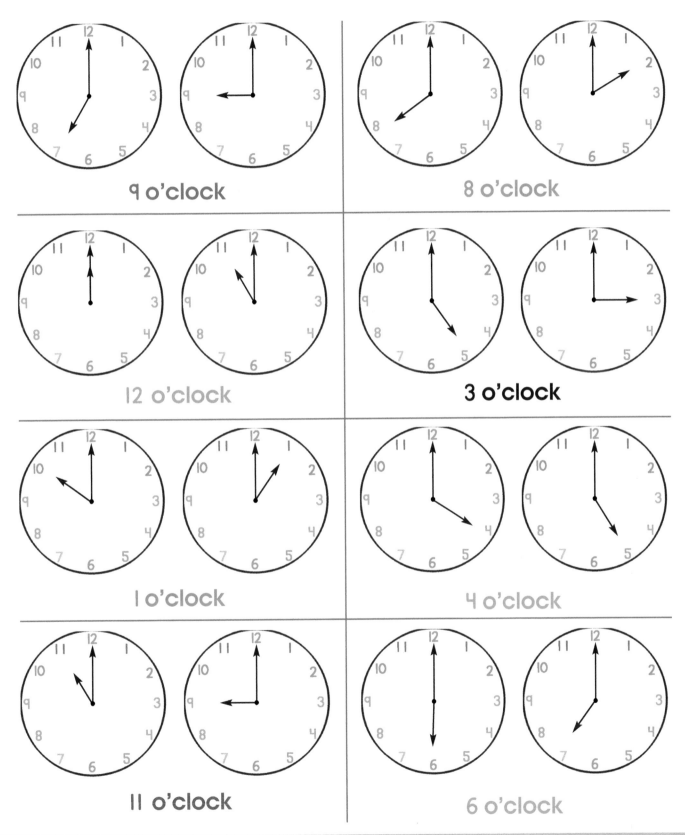

9 o'clock

8 o'clock

12 o'clock

3 o'clock

1 o'clock

4 o'clock

11 o'clock

6 o'clock

Complete the clocks by filling in the missing numbers.
Tell what time each clock is showing.

What time are the clock showing?

_____   _____   _____
      A   B   C

TELLING TIME TO THE HALF HOUR

$\frac{1}{2}$ hour time

60 minutes make one hour. When the long hand is on six the time is half past the hour. Look at the clock. The long hand (minute hand) points to 6. The short hand is mid-way between 3 and 4. The time is half past three or three thirty 3:30.

When the long hand (minute hand) points to 6, it is half past the hour.

Activity:

What time is it?

Half past ☐ or ☐

Half past ☐ or ☐

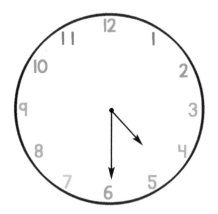

Half past ☐ or ☐

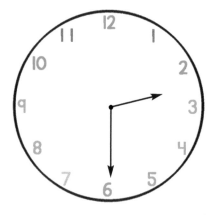

Half past ☐ or ☐

Draw hands to show these times.

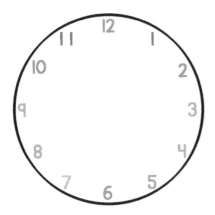

1. **Half past 9 or 9:30**

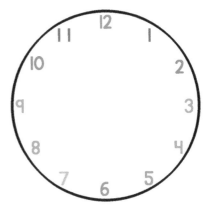

4. **Half past 7 or 7:30**

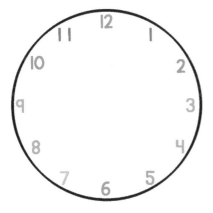

2. **Half past 1 or 1:30**

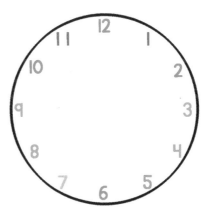

5. **Half past 8 or 8:30**

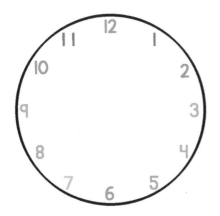

3. **Half past 12 or 12:30**

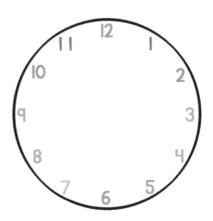

6. **Half past 2 or 2:30**

Draw hands to show the times.

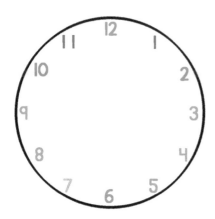

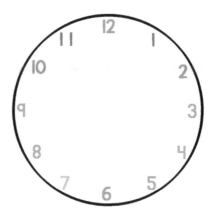

7. **Half past 10 or 10:30**

10. **Half past 6 or 6:30**

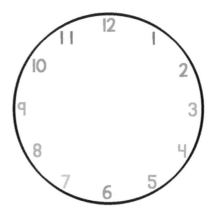

8. **Half past 3 or 3:30**

11. **Half past 5 or 5:30**

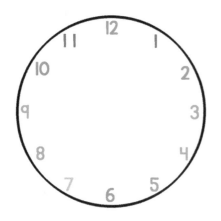

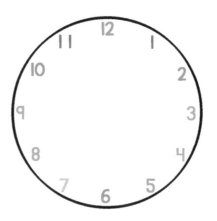

9. **Half past 11 or 11:30**

12. **Half past 4 or 4:30**

I Can Count

NUMERALS AND
THEIR NUMBER NAMES: 30 – 50

Draw objects in the spaces to match the numerals.

30	oooooooooooooooo ooooooooooooooooo	**thirty**
31		**thirty-one**
32		**thirty-two**
33		**thirty-three**
34		**thirty-four**
35		**thirty-five**
36		**thirty-six**
37		**thirty-seven**

NUMERALS AND THEIR NUMBER NAMES

Draw small circles in the spaces to match the numerals.

38		thirty-eight
39		thirty-nine
40		forty
41		forty-one
42		forty-two
43		forty-three
44		forty-four
45		forty-five
46		forty-six
47		forty-seven
48		forty-eight
49		forty-nine
50		fifty

Fill in the boxes with numerals 1 to 50 counting backwards.

50	49			
				41
40				36
		33		
		28		
25				
	19			
			12	
			7	

Trace the numerals from 1 to 50

1	2	3	4	5
6	7	8	9	10
11	12	13	14	15
16	17	18	19	20
21	22	23	24	25
26	27	28	29	30
31	32	33	34	35
36	37	38	39	40
41	42	43	44	45
46	47	48	49	50

Measurement

MEASURING LIQUIDS

Liquids are measured in litres.

Estimate and Verify Capacity.

The large milk carton holds as much as _____ small boxes.

The jug holds as much as _____ glasses.

How much will it take to fill the larger one?

jug

bucket

guess: _____ jugs

measure: _____ jugs

glass

soda bottle

guess: _____ glasses

measure: _____ glasses

tablespoon

soup bowl

guess: _____ table-spoons

measure: _____ table-spoons

pitcher

cup

guess: _____ cups

measure: _____ cups

Measurement - Capacity

I can pour things
into this jug.

I cannot pour
anything into this.

Mark the objects that I can pour things into.

Full/Empty

This glass is full.

This glass is empty.

Mark which ones are full.

OBJECTIVE: Tell which contatiner holds more or less.

Capacity

Which holds more? Mark it with X.

Which holds less? Mark it with X.

Capacity

Which holds more? Circle the one which holds more.

Measurement

Measuring parts of the body in centimetres

Get a piece of cord and a ruler to measure certain parts of your body.

Parts of the body	Length in cm
arm's length	_____ centimetres
waist	_____ centimetres
head	_____ centimetres
length of hand	_____ centimetres
hand span	_____ centimetres

My height is _____ centimetres.

My stride when walking is _____ centimetres.

LET US READ

The Thermometer

The thermometer is an instrument that is used to take the temperature of a person. Temperature tells us how hot or cold a thing is. The thermometer gives us this information in degrees Celsius (°C). A person's normal body temperature is 37.5°C. The thermometer can also tell us the temperature of the day.

MEASUREMENT

Tell the temperatures on these thermometers.

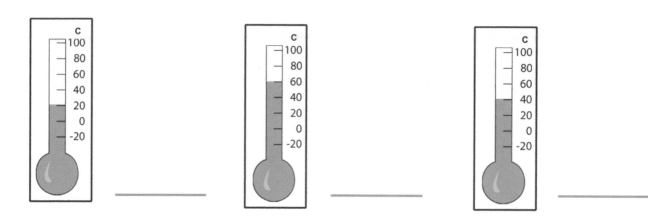

_____   _____   _____

Measuring Length with non-standard units

We can use the following methods to measure length.

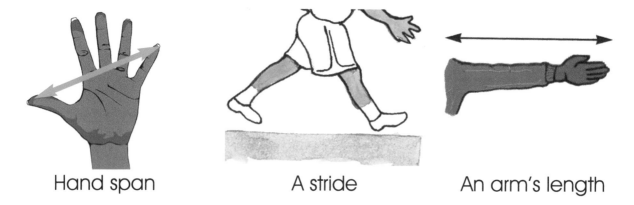

Hand span   A stride   An arm's length

Measure the objects in your classroom using non-standard units.

1. The length of my desk is _____ hand spans.

2. The length of my teacher's desk is _____ hand spans.

3. The length of the class whiteboard is _____ arm spans.

4. The length of one wall of the classroom is _____ strides.

WHAT ARE WE USED FOR?

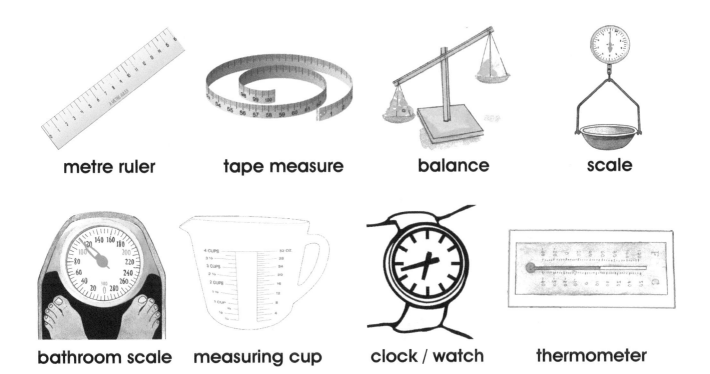

metre ruler   tape measure   balance   scale

bathroom scale   measuring cup   clock / watch   thermometer

Which instrument do we use to measure...

1. how heavy or light a person is? _____

2. a piece of yam? _____

3. items for baking a cake? _____

4. a person's waist? _____

5. a person's temperature? _____

6. the time of day? _____

LET'S LEARN THE DAYS OF THE WEEK IN SPANISH

domingo	Sunday
lunes	Monday
martes	Tuesday
miércoles	**Wednesday**
jueves	Thursday
viernes	**Friday**
sábado	Saturday

I Can Count

NUMERALS AND THEIR NUMBER NAMES: 50 – 70

Draw objects in the spaces to match the numerals.

50	ooooooooooooooooooo ooooooooooooooooo ooooooooooooooooo	fifty
51		fifty-one
52		fifty-two
53		fifty-three
54		fifty-four
55		fifty-five
56		fifty-six
57		fifty-seven

Draw objects in the spaces to match the numerals.

58		fifty-eight
59		fifty-nine
60		sixty
61		sixty-one
62		sixty-two
63		sixty-three
64		sixty-four
65		sixty-five
66		sixty-six
67		sixty-seven
68		sixty-eight
69		sixty-nine
70		seventy

Counting forward, numbers 1 to 70.

1				5	6	7
8		10				14
			18			
						28
36						
						49
			53			
	58					
				68		

Counting backwards 70 to 1

						64
63			60			
		54				50
						43
35		33				
28			25			22
						15
			11			
	6					1

Addition

LET US READ

The number that is 1 more than 2 is 3, while the number that is 1 more than 7 is 8.

In each case we are adding 1 to the number.

Example: + =

$$2 \quad + \quad 1 \quad = \quad 3$$

Add one to the following numbers and write the number names.

1. 3 _____
2. 57 _____
3. 10 _____
4. 16 _____

5. 44 _____
6. 68 _____
7. 52 _____
8. 31 _____

9. 0 _____
10. 64 _____
11. 35 _____
12. 12 _____

LET US READ

1. Tom has 12 apples. He adds 3 more apples to what he has. How many apples does Tom have now?

   _____

2. Bob has 19 marbles. How many is 1 marble more than what Bob has?

   _____

3. Sue has 15 pineapples. Jack has 1 more pineapple than Sue. How many pineapples does Jack have?

   _____

4. Andrew has 9 mangoes. His sister Anna gave him 9 more mangoes. Andrew now has how many mangoes?

   _____

5. Wanda has 12 dolls. Terry has 2 more dolls than Wanda. How many dolls does Terry have?

   _____

6. Peter has 8 sweets. Sammy has 4 sweets. Altogether they have?

   _____

7. I have 10 birds and I decided to buy 3 more birds. How many birds will I have now?

   _____

THINK ABOUT IT.

Answer the following questions.

a. Billy has nineteen toy cars. His father bought one more for him. How many toy cars in all does Billy have?

b. Sue has 0 kittens. She went to the pet store and bought four kittens. How many kittens does Sue have now?

c. Jack has 7 hats. He went to the store and saw a pretty hat and he bought it. How many hats does Jack have now that he bought one more?

Answer the following questions.

a. Pam has 8 pencils. Her mother gave her 7 more. How many pencils does Pam have in all?

b. Peter has 15 marbles. His brother gave him four more. How many marbles does Peter have altogether?

c. Mary has 13 books in her bag already. She added one more book to her bag. How many books does Mary have now?

d. Jack has 18 sweets. He went to the store and bought two more. How many sweets does Jack have in all?

ADDITION

Find the missing numbers.

8 + _____ = 10   2 + _____ = 10

3 + _____ = 10   7 + _____ = 10

5 + _____ = 10   5 + _____ = 10

10 + _____ = 10   0 + _____ = 10

1 + _____ = 10   9 + _____ = 10

Do these.

(a) 9 + 9 = _____   (b) 7 + 3 = _____   (c) 2 + 8 = _____

(d) 4 + 5 = _____   (e) 8 + 1 = _____   (f) 0 + 9 = _____

(g) 6 + 3 = _____   (h) 5 + 3 = _____   (i) 7 + 8 = _____

(j) 8 + 8 = _____   (k) 9 + 6 = _____   (l) 8 + 5 = _____

(m) 1 + 7 = _____   (n) 4 + 9 = _____   (o) 7 + 7 = _____

(p) 4 + 0 = _____   (q) 6 + 6 = _____   (r) 2 + 7 = _____

What number when added to 3 gives thirteen?

$$\boxed{} + 3 = 13$$

The number that can be added to 3 to get thirteen is ten. Let us check to see.

$$\boxed{10} + 3 = 13$$

Fill in the missing numbers.

(a) $\boxed{} + 3 = 5$ (b) $\boxed{} + 8 = 20$ (c) $\boxed{} + 8 = 20$

(d) $7 + \boxed{} = 20$ (e) $4 + \boxed{} = 17$ (f) $\boxed{} + 4 = 20$

(g) $\boxed{} + 8 = 15$ (h) $\boxed{} + 9 = 20$ (i) $19 + \boxed{} = 29$

(j) $8 + \boxed{} = 10$ (k) $8 + \boxed{} = 16$ (l) $18 + \boxed{} = 20$

(m) $\boxed{} + 15 = 15$ (n) $\boxed{} + 13 = 20$ (o) $\boxed{} + 15 = 20$

OBJECTIVE: Add without carrying a remainder.

We put the numbers in their correct places, that is, ones in the ones place and tens in the tens place. When adding we first add the numbers in the ones column, then next we move to the tens column. Look at the following steps.

Step 1

Step 2

Add the following. Pay attention to the place value.

```
  1 2          4          1 8            1
+   4        + 1 2      +   1        + 1 8
_____        _____      _____        _____
```

```
  5          1 4          1 5            0
+ 1 4        +   5      +   0        + 1 5
_____        _____      _____        _____
```

Add the following. Pay attention to the place value.

```
  1 2          1 4          1 8          1 1
+ 1 4        + 1 2        + 1 1        + 1 8
_____        _____        _____        _____
```

```
  1 5          1 4          1 5          1 5
+ 1 4        + 1 5        + 1 0        + 1 5
_____        _____        _____        _____
```

If after adding the numbers in the ones column, the result is greater than nine, rename to tens and ones. Add the new tens to the tens column. Look at the steps below for a clearer understanding.

Step 1

$$\begin{array}{r} ① \\ 2\ 4 \\ +1\ 8 \\ \hline 2 \end{array}$$

Step 2

$$\begin{array}{r} 2\ 4 \\ +1\ 8 \\ \hline 4\ 2 \end{array}$$

After adding 8 and four together we get 12. Observe that the entire number twelve is not placed under the ones column. Instead, the two ones are placed under the ones column and one ten is carried over to the tens column to be added to the other tens. So, 2 tens plus 1 ten plus one more ten give 4 tens.

Add the following numbers. See if you can observe any pattern. Pay attention to your tens and ones. Check yourself.

$$\begin{array}{r} 5 \\ +\ 1\ 5 \\ \hline \end{array} \qquad \begin{array}{r} 1\ 5 \\ +\ \ 5 \\ \hline \end{array} \qquad \begin{array}{r} 1\ 8 \\ +\ \ 2 \\ \hline \end{array} \qquad \begin{array}{r} 2 \\ +\ 1\ 8 \\ \hline \end{array}$$

$$\begin{array}{r} 1\ 5 \\ +\ \ 6 \\ \hline \end{array} \qquad \begin{array}{r} 6 \\ +\ 1\ 5 \\ \hline \end{array} \qquad \begin{array}{r} 1\ 5 \\ +\ \ 9 \\ \hline \end{array} \qquad \begin{array}{r} 9 \\ +\ 1\ 5 \\ \hline \end{array}$$

$$\begin{array}{r} 5 \\ +\ 1\ 7 \\ \hline \end{array} \qquad \begin{array}{r} 1\ 7 \\ +\ \ 5 \\ \hline \end{array} \qquad \begin{array}{r} 1\ 6 \\ +\ \ 4 \\ \hline \end{array} \qquad \begin{array}{r} 4 \\ +\ 1\ 6 \\ \hline \end{array}$$

Adding Vertically.

$$\begin{array}{r} 3 \\ + \ 4 \\ \hline \end{array}$$

$$\begin{array}{r} 7 \\ + \ 2 \\ \hline \end{array}$$

$$\begin{array}{r} 5 \\ + \ 0 \\ \hline \end{array}$$

$$\begin{array}{r} 3 \\ + \ 3 \\ \hline \end{array}$$

$$\begin{array}{r} 5 \\ + \ 5 \\ \hline \end{array}$$

$$\begin{array}{r} 6 \\ + \ 4 \\ \hline \end{array}$$

Adding Horizontally.

    $2 + 4 =$

    $5 + 5 =$

 $4 + 1 =$

    $3 + 3 =$

 $5 + 2 =$

Addition without carrying.

Example: 70 + 10 =

Step 1:   Add the Ones.

        0 + 0 = 0

Step 2:   Add the Tens.

        7 + 1 = 8

8 goes in the Tens place.

        70 + 10 = 80

Add the following:

1.	Tens	Ones
	2	3
+	2	3

2.	Tens	Ones
	2	2
+	3	6

3.	Tens	Ones
	2	6
+	0	3

4.	Tens	Ones
	8	7
+	1	2

5.

Tens	Ones
9	7
+ 6	2

6.

Tens	Ones
2	3
+ 2	3

7.

Tens	Ones
5	0
+ 1	0

8.

Tens	Ones
6	1
+ 2	1

9.

Tens	Ones
8	5
+ 1	4

10.

Tens	Ones
1	4
+ 7	4

11.

Tens	Ones
7	8
+ 1	1

12.

Tens	Ones
5	6
+ 1	2

LET US READ

Always look for the words, in all **and** altogether **because they will tell you to** add.

For example:

1. **There are** 8 **boys and** 6 **girls on the bus. How many children are on the bus altogether?**
   8 boys + 6 girls = 14 children

2. **Danny had** 7 **apples. His father gave him** 3 **more apples. How many apples does Danny have in all?**
   7 apples + 3 apples = 10 apples

Now do these.

3. Students of class IC ate 4 hamburgers, 10 hot dogs and 3 patties for lunch. How many items in all did they eat?

_____

4. 6 women and 4 men work on my father's farm. How many people altogether work on the farm?

_____

5. I see 9 teachers in the class talking. Here come 3 more teachers to join in. How many teachers altogether are there now?

_____

6. John ate 2 patties. Nicole ate 1 patty. The rest of the students ate 8 patties. How many patties in all were eaten?

_____

7. 12 boys and 3 girls from grade 1C came to school today. How many students in all were present in class today?

_____

8. I bought a slice of cake for $3.00, a donut for $1.00 and a juice for $5.00. How much money in all did I spend?

_____

9. Alicia collected 12 bottle caps. Tanya collected 8 bottle caps. How many bottle caps have they collected altogether?

_____

10. Mom bought me 10 gold fish. Dad bought me 7 more gold fish. How many gold fish in all do I have?

_____

11. In a basket there are 13 June plums. A woman added 13 more June plums to the basket. How many June plums in all are there?

_____

12. I bought 12 bananas. I also bought 3 grapefruits. How many fruits did I buy altogether?

_____

THINK ABOUT IT

1. Nicole made 16 cupcakes. Her mother baked 8 cupcakes. How many cupcakes were made?

    _____

2. My dad gave me 8 stamps. I had 12 stamps before. How many stamps do I have now?

    _____

3. Mother has 10 chickens. Uncle Bill gave her 10 more chickens. How many chickens does she have now?

    _____

4. Kenneth had 35¢. His father gave him 15¢ more. How many cents has Kenneth now?

    _____

5. John has 13 marbles. Romesh has 15 marbles. How many marbles do they have altogether?

    _____

NUMBER – NUMBER OPERATIONS

Use the number line 0 - 20 to show addition.

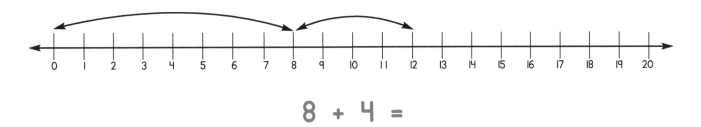

$$8 + 4 =$$

We use the number line to solve this problem by beginning at 0 then moving to 8 on the line. Next we move 4 places to the right counting on to 4 in ones. We stop at 12.

$$8 + 4 = 12$$

Complete each number sentence. Show the addition using the number line. Draw a number line 0 - 20 for each problem.

⟵————————————————————————⟶

1. 6 + 4 = _____

⟵————————————————————————⟶

2. 10 + 6 = _____

3. $9 + 5 =$ _____

4. $9 + 9 =$ _____

5. $8 + 8 =$ _____

6. $10 + 2 =$ _____

7. $9 + 3 =$ _____

8. $4 + 4 =$ _____

Adding numbers horizontally

Let's look at this problem.

a. $15 + 3 = \boxed{}$

One of these numbers is smaller than the others.
I count on from 15 to 3 more.

15, 16, 17, 18 $15 + 3 = \boxed{18}$

b. $3 + 16 = \boxed{}$

One of the numbers is small. Start with the bigger number.

Count on from 16 to 3 more.

16, 17, 18, 19 $3 + 16 = \boxed{19}$

Solve these problems by counting on.

1. $4 + 9 = \boxed{}$ 7. $3 + 12 = \boxed{}$

2. $10 + 8 = \boxed{}$ 8. $20 + 10 = \boxed{}$

3. $8 + 3 = \boxed{}$ 9. $20 + 10 = \boxed{}$

4. $4 + 19 = \boxed{}$ 10. $10 + 10 = \boxed{}$

5. $22 + 3 = \boxed{}$ 11. $3 + 17 = \boxed{}$

6. $4 + 15 = \boxed{}$ 12. $18 + 4 = \boxed{}$

Now do these.

1. $10 + 6 =$ _____

2. $4 + 12 =$ _____

3. $9 + 9 =$ _____

4. $15 + 8 =$ _____

5. $5 + 6 =$ _____

6. $7 + 14 =$ _____

7. $6 + 6 =$ _____

8. $6 + 4 =$ _____

9. $15 + 5 =$ _____

10. $9 + 3 =$ _____

11. $8 + 4 =$ _____

12. $4 + 5 =$ _____

13. $3 + 6 =$ _____

14. $12 + 2 =$ _____

15. $10 + 3 =$ _____

16. $10 + 5 =$ _____

Repeated Addition, Making 'Sets of'

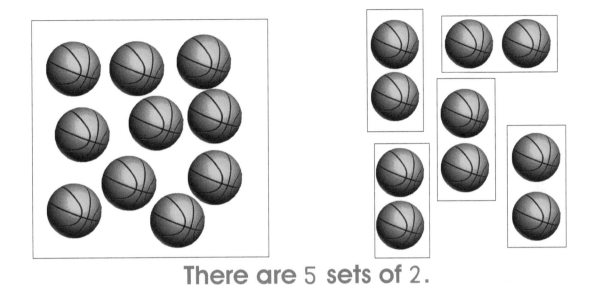

There are 5 sets of 2.

Mark sets of 2.

There are _____ sets of 2.   There are _____ sets of 2.

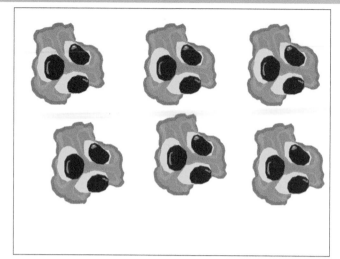

There are _____ sets of 2.

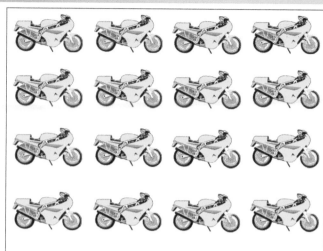

There are _____ sets of 2.

There are _____ sets of 2.

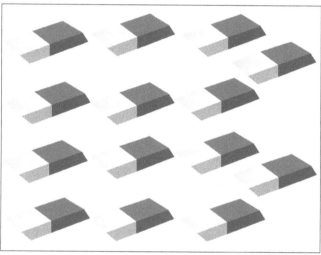

There are _____ sets of 2.

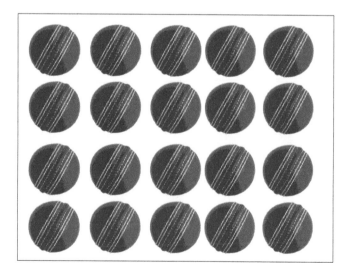

There are _____ sets of 2.

There are _____ sets of 2.

OBJECTIVE: Use >, < to tell the true value of the number.

Complete the following:

1. 8 + 3 = _____

2. 5 + 6 = _____

3. 10 + 5 = _____

4. 7 + 6 = _____

5. 12 + 2 = _____

6. 9 + 4 = _____

7. 2 + 9 = _____

8. 10 + 1 = _____

9. 5 + 4 = _____

10. 5 + 6 = _____

Make the statements true by putting > or < in the boxes.

1. 15 ☐ 11

2. 8 ☐ 9

3. 7 ☐ 8

4. 13 ☐ 16

5. 14 ☐ 12

6. 12 ☐ 13

7. 10 ☐ 11

8. 18 ☐ 10

9. 16 ☐ 17

10. 5 ☐ 3

11. 17 ☐ 20

12. 2 ☐ 4

13. 19 ☐ 17

14. 6 ☐ 9

15. 20 ☐ 16

16. 18 ☐ 16

ADDITION

1. Henry had 10¢ (cents). His mother gave him 15¢ (cents). How many cents does he now have?

_____

2. Gabrielle brought 7 flowers to school. Her friend, Josie, brought 7 flowers. How many flowers have they altogether?

_____

3. Paul had 16 stamps. His friend gave him 12 more. How many stamps does Paul now have?

_____

4. 6 dogs were fighting in the street. Soon 4 more dogs were fighting in the street. How many dogs were fighting in the street?

_____

Shapes

I am a circle.

I am round.

I have no sides.

I can roll.

I am a square.

A square is a figure with 4 equal sides.

A square cannot roll.

I am a triangle.

I have three sides.

I cannot roll.

I am a rectangle.

I have 4 sides, two short sides and two long sides.

I cannot roll. Why?

Because of my edges.

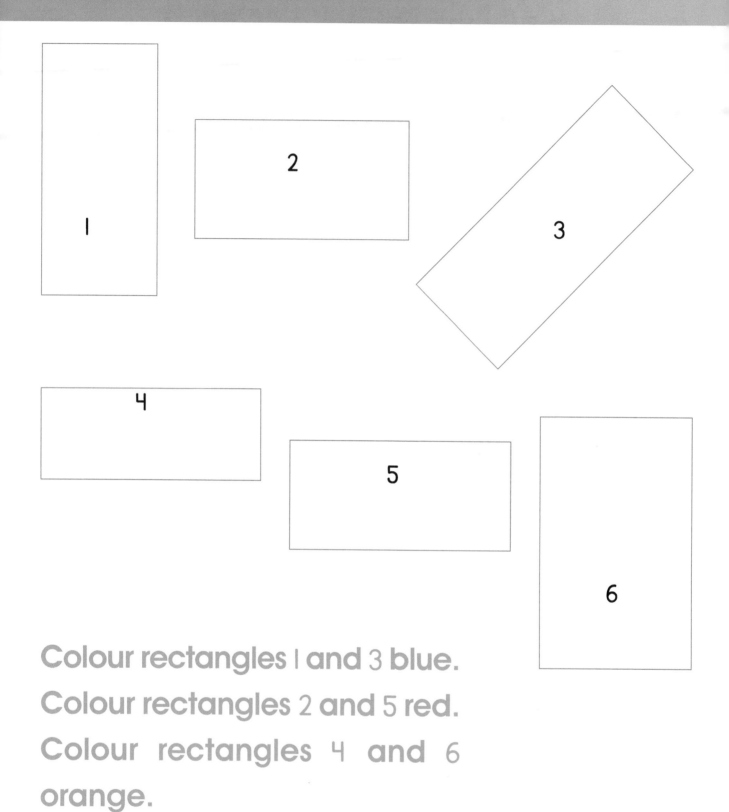

Colour rectangles 1 and 3 blue.

Colour rectangles 2 and 5 red.

Colour rectangles 4 and 6 orange.

Colour the squares and tell me how many there are. _____

Colour the circles blue. Say how many there are. _____

Study and trace these shapes. Colour them.

These are circles.

These are squares. A square has 4 equal sides.

These are triangles.. A triangle has 3 sides.

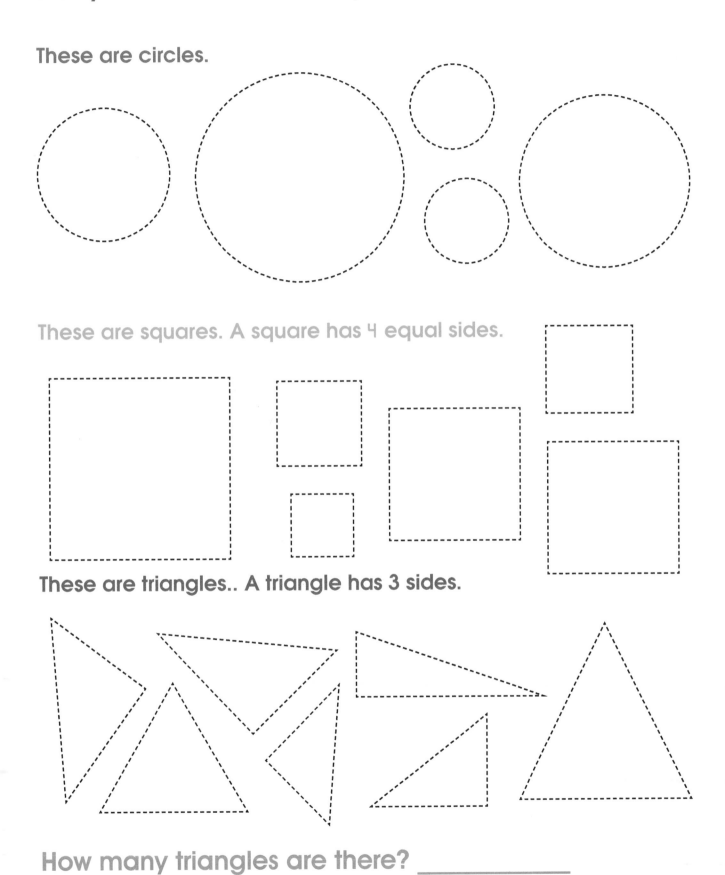

How many triangles are there? _____

Look around your classroom and draw the shapes that you see. Discuss these shapes with your class-mates.

Look around your home and community and draw the shapes that you see.

What things do you see with more than one shape? What shapes do they have?

Use the drawing tools of the computer to draw pictures using the four basic shapes: circle, square, rectangle, triangle.

Match the shapes to their names.

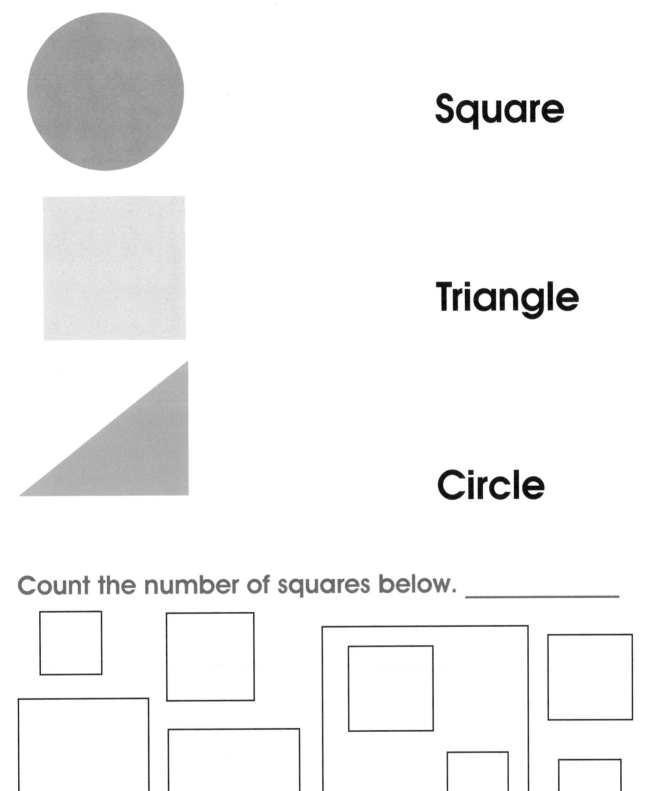

Square

Triangle

Circle

Count the number of squares below. _____

THE CUBE

This is a cube. A cube has edges.

The edges of the cube keep it from rolling.

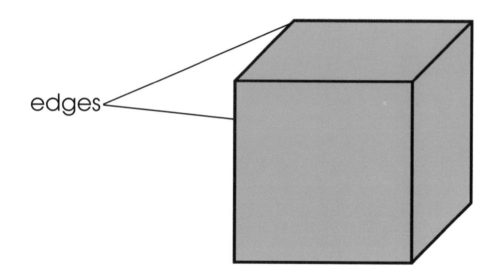

A cube also has faces.

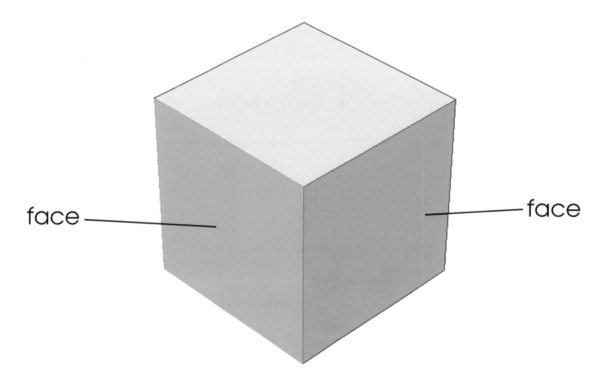

OBJECTIVE: Identify objects in the environment that have a solid shape.

Circle the cubes.

The shape of the face of the cube is called a square.

Join the dots to make squares.

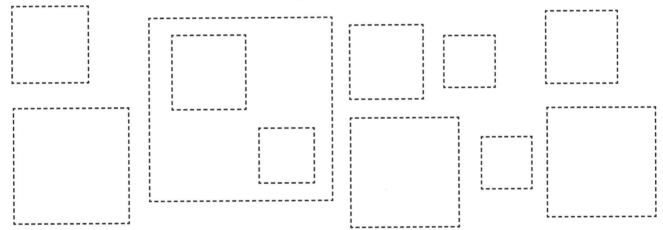

Circle the squares.

THE SPHERE

A sphere rolls very easily in any direction. A sphere has one face only.

OBJECTIVE: Identify objects in the environment that have a solid shape.

Mark the spheres with an X.

The shadow of the sphere is called a circle.

Join the dots to form circles.

IDENTIFYING THE CUBOID

edges

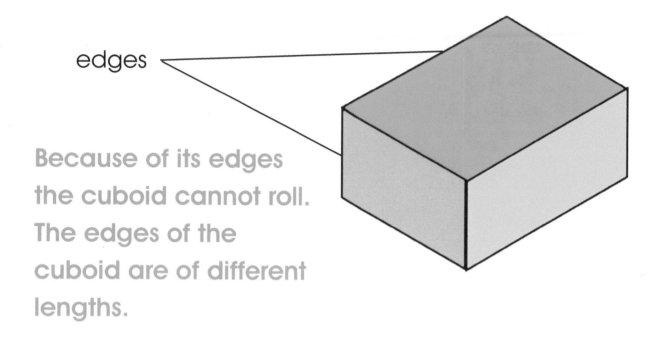

Because of its edges the cuboid cannot roll. The edges of the cuboid are of different lengths.

Mark the edges of these cuboids.

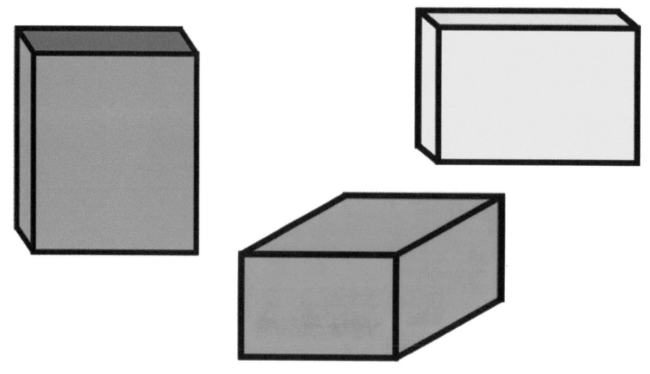

The edges of cuboids have different lengths.

A cuboid has 6 faces. The faces of the cuboid are of different sizes.

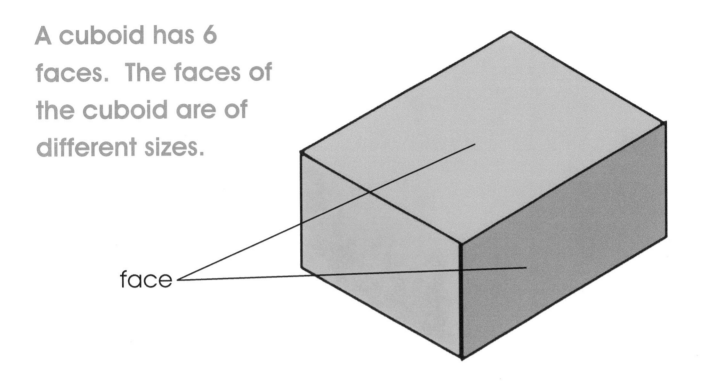

face

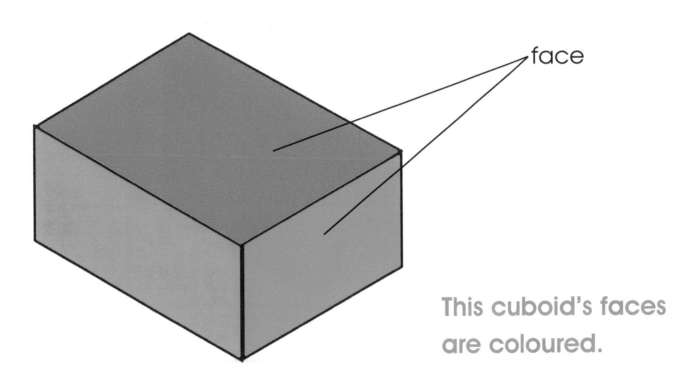

face

This cuboid's faces are coloured.

GEOMETRY: KNOW YOUR SHAPES.

Solids

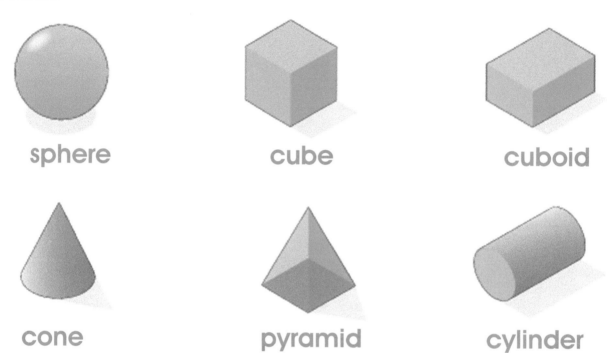

sphere   cube   cuboid

cone   pyramid   cylinder

Use an X to mark which solids are exactly alike.

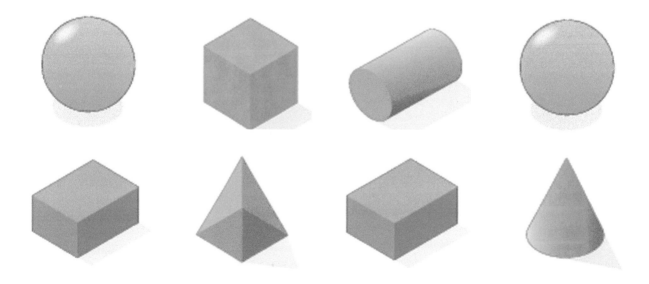

Which solid is exactly alike to the first solid? Mark it with an X.

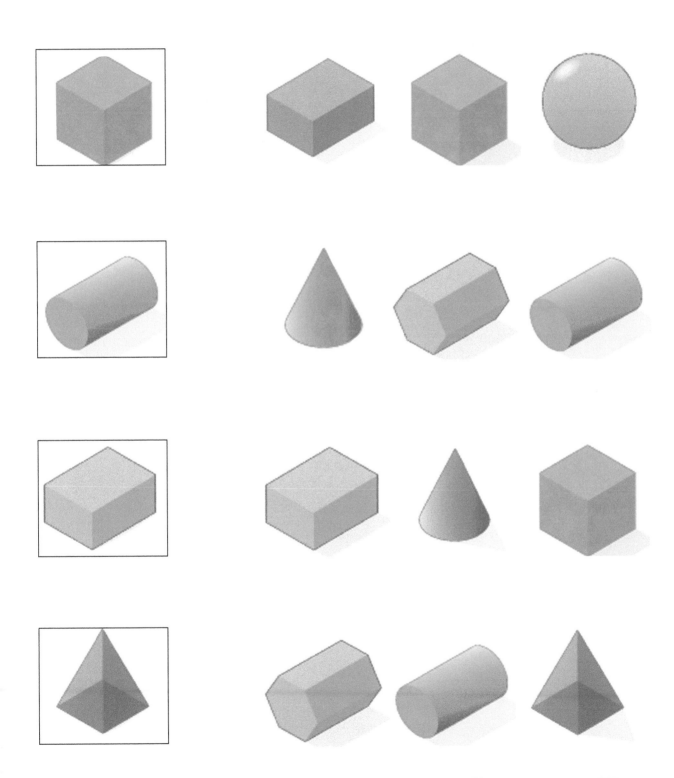

OBJECTIVE: Identify and draw the missing shapes to complete patterns.

PATTERNS

Complete the patterns.

1.

2.

3. **What comes next?**

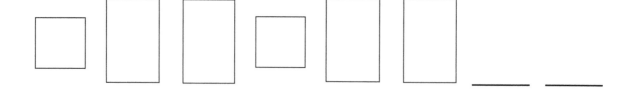

1. Complete the number patterns.
   Choose a number from the numbers in the box.

   12, 22, 12, 22, _____, 22, 12, 22,

   24,   12,   22

2. Complete the number patterns.

   8, 12, 8, 12, , 8, _____, 8, 12, 8

   73, 4, 4, 73, 4, 4, 73, _____, _____

Shape Patterns.

The pattern is small big, small big...

Change in colour

The pattern is red green, red green, ...

Change in shape

The pattern is triangle, square, star, triangle, square, star, ...

Activity

1. Describe the pattern.

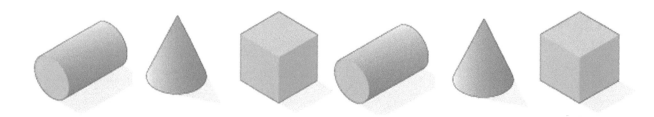

The pattern is cylinder, _____, _____, ...

2. Draw and colour the missing shape in the pattern.

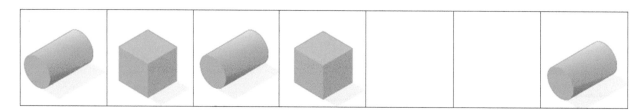

The Number Line

Using the number line 0 to 20 to show addition.

Example: 5 + 5 = [?]

We first begin by starting at 0 then move to 5.

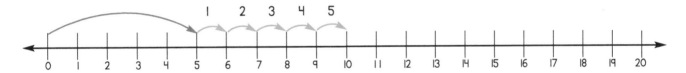

In the next step we move 5 places to the right counting on to 5 in ones. We stop at 10.

Complete the number sentences and show the addition on the number line.

16 + 4 = [ ]

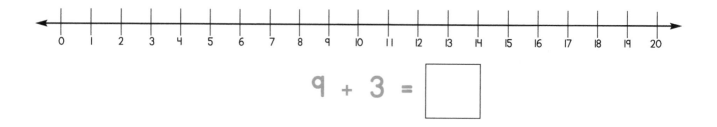

$$9 + 3 = \boxed{}$$

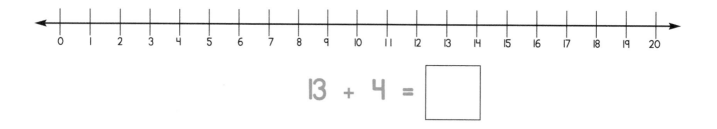

$$13 + 4 = \boxed{}$$

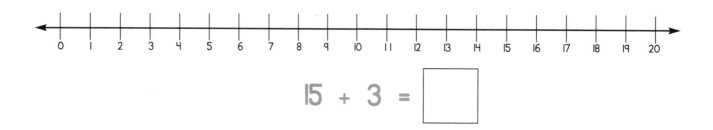

$$15 + 3 = \boxed{}$$

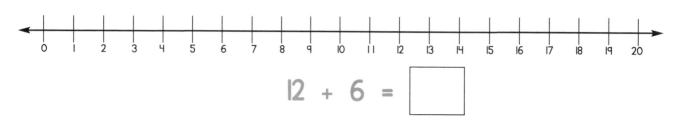

$$12 + 6 = \boxed{}$$

Adding numbers horizontally without renaming.

Example: 13 + 6 = [?]

When one of the numbers is small begin counting on from the larger number. In this case, count on from 13 to 6 more.

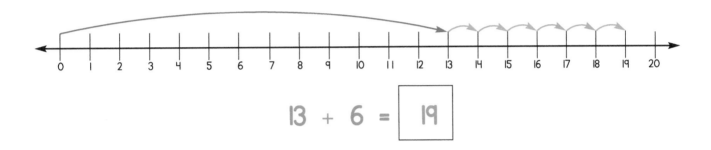

$$13 + 6 = \boxed{19}$$

Example: 4 + 10 = ?

Start with the bigger number because one of the numbers is small. Count on from 10 to 4 more.

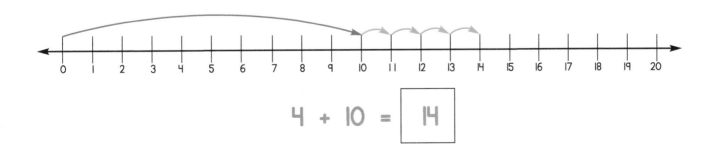

$$4 + 10 = \boxed{14}$$

Now do these by counting on.

1. 17 + 2 = _____

2. 15 + 3 = _____

3. 3 + 11 = _____

4. 16 + 2 = _____

5. 14 + 2 = _____

6. 13 + 4 = _____

7. 15 + 4 = _____

8. 20 + 2 = _____

9. 13 + 6 = _____

10. 13 + 5 = _____

11. 11 + 5 = _____

12. 5 + 24 = _____

13. 28 + 1 = _____

14. 14 + 5 = _____

15. 12 + 7 = _____

16. 3 + 12 = _____

17. 10 + 7 = _____

18. 34 + 2 = _____

19. 31 + 6 = _____

20. 18 + 0 = _____

ADDING ON THE NUMBER LINE.

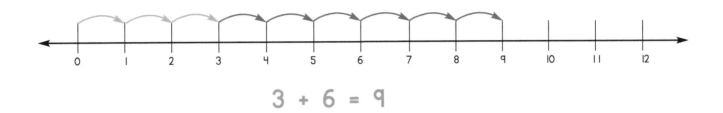

$$3 + 6 = 9$$

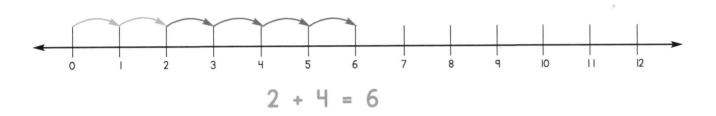

$$2 + 4 = 6$$

Draw number lines 0 to 12 in your exercise books and use them to find your answers.

1. $7 + 3 = $ _____
2. $6 + 2 = $ _____
3. $9 + 3 = $ _____
4. $4 + 5 = $ _____
5. $8 + 3 = $ _____

6. $3 + 4 = $ _____
7. $7 + 5 = $ _____
8. $7 + 4 = $ _____
9. $4 + 4 = $ _____
10. $5 + 5 = $ _____

SUBTRACTING ON THE NUMBER LINE.

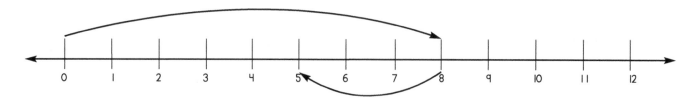

$$8 - 3 = 5$$

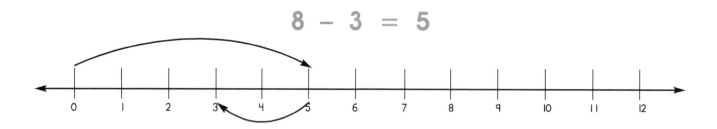

$$5 - 2 = 3$$

Draw a number line 0 to 12 and use it to find your answers.

1. $11 - 3 =$ _____

2. $8 - 2 =$ _____

3. $5 - 3 =$ _____

4. $10 - 5 =$ _____

5. $10 - 3 =$ _____

6. $8 - 4 =$ _____

7. $12 - 5 =$ _____

8. $10 - 4 =$ _____

9. $7 - 4 =$ _____

10. $9 - 5 =$ _____

Counting by 2s, 3s, 4s and 5s

COUNTING BY 2s.

OBJECTIVE: Count by 2, 3, 4 and 5.

How many? Write the answer in the box.

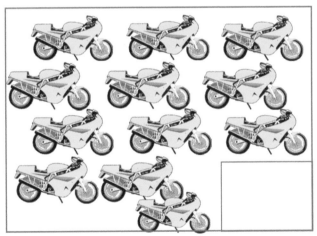

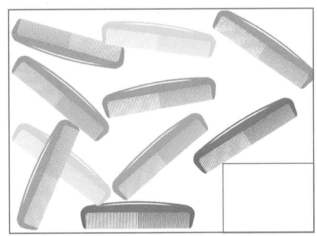

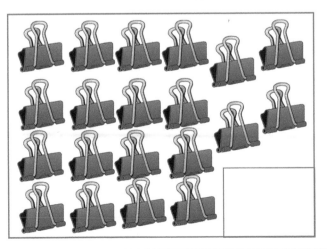

COUNTING BY 3s.

How many? Write the answer in the box.

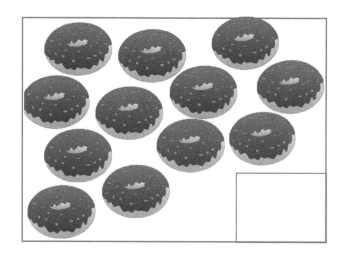

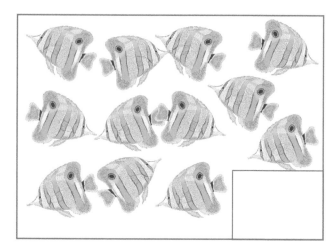

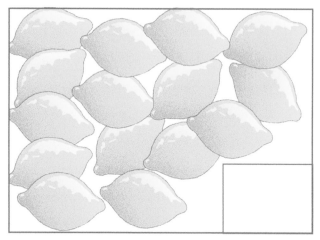

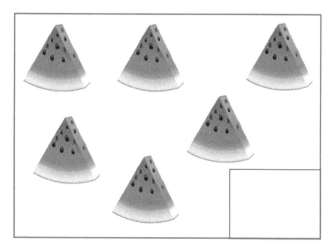

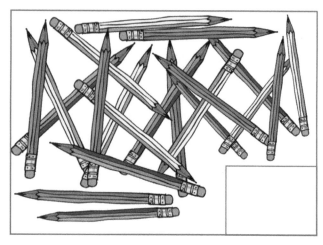

COUNTING BY 4s.

How many? Write the answer in the box.

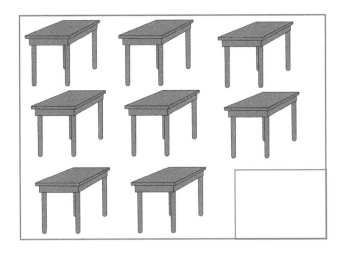

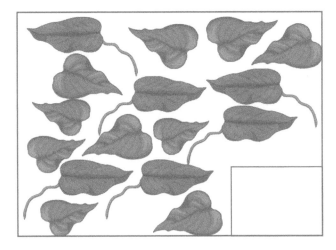

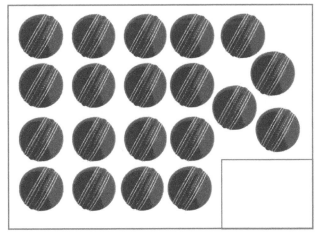

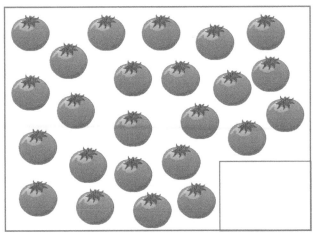

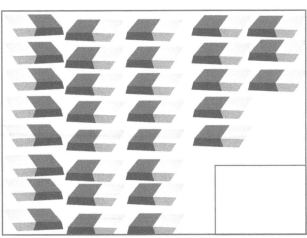

COUNTING BY 5s.

How many? Write the answer in the box.

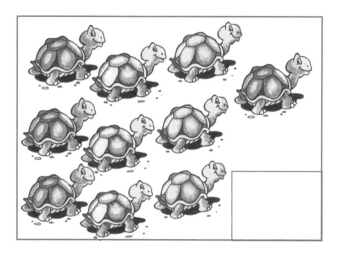

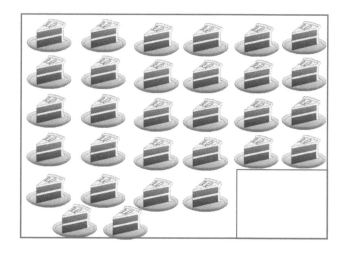

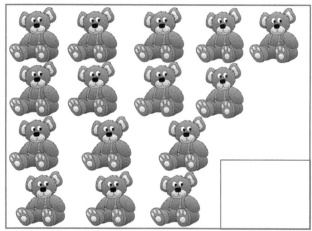

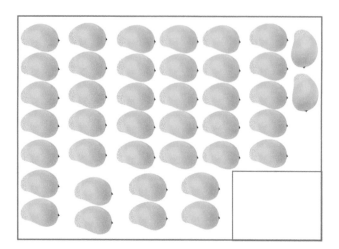

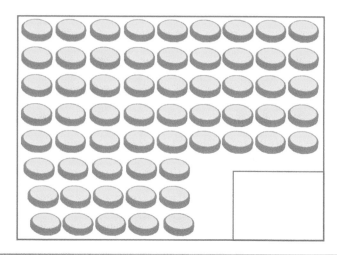

Gathering Data

TALLY CHARTS/SHEETS

These are charts/sheets which are used to show important information. Each stroke | represents I object or I person and four strokes + one stroke across the four strokes ||||| represent 5 objects or 5 persons.

Grade IC Students' Favourite Cartoons

NAMES	TALLY STROKES	TOTAL How many?
Sesame Street	||||| ||||| |||||	15
Dora the Explorer	||||| ||||| ||	12
Sponge Bob Square Pants	||||| ||||| ||	12
Ni Hao Kai-lan	||||| ||||| |||	13

CLASSIFYING OBJECTS

Tallying

Classifying objects according to colour.

How many coloured caps?

blue (8), red (6), green (4), yellow (5), brown (2).

To show 5 on the tally chart we make 4 strokes down and 1 stroke across the four strokes.

For example: **||||** = 5

CAPS/COLOUR	TALLY STROKES	TOTAL How many?
blue cap	|||| |||	8
red cap		
green cap		
yellow cap		
brown cap		

CLASSIFYING OBJECTS ACCORDING TO SHAPE.

Shapes: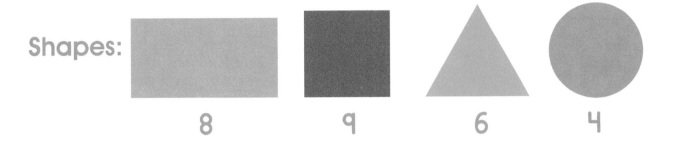

| 8 | 9 | 6 | 4 |

SHAPES	TALLY STROKES	TOTAL How many?

Classification

We can collect objects and classify them by their shape, their colour, their texture and so on.

Complete the following. The first one is done for you.

OBJECT	TALLY STROKES	TOTAL
8 objects	ⅢⅠ Ⅲ	8
9 objects		
12 objects		
6 objects		
15 objects		
11 objects		
10 objects		
4 objects		
0 objects		
5 objects		

Counting the number in each classification (tallying)

10 starapples, 12 mangoes, 8 pineapples, 9 grapes, 7 star fruits.

FRUITS	TALLY STROKES	TOTAL How many?
grapes		9
mangoes		12
pineapples		8
starapples		10
star fruits		7

Complete this tally table.

8 cabbages, 7 cucumbers, 12 cho-chos, 13 carrots

VEGETABLES	TALLY STROKES	TOTAL How many?
cabbages		
cho-chos		
carrots		
cucumbers		

VAMOS A CONTAR EN EL ESPAÑOL.

(Let's Count in Spanish)

uno	dos	tres	cuatro	cinco	seis	siete	ocho	nueve	diez

1   2   3   4   5   6   7   8   9   10

uno   dos   tres   cuatro   cinco   seis   siete   ocho   nueve   diez

OBJECTIVE: Collect, organize and interpret information in practical situations.

GRAPHS

Pupils of class IR were told to bring their favourite pets to school. Here are the pets that were brought to school.

Count the number of pets that each pupil brought to school.

LIST OF PETS	NUMBER OF PUPILS	TOTAL
dog	🐕🐕🐕🐕🐕🐕🐕🐕🐕🐕	10
guinea pig	🐹🐹🐹🐹🐹	
fish	🐠🐠	
bird	🐦🐦🐦🐦🐦	
hamster	🐹🐹🐹🐹	
cat	🐈🐈🐈🐈🐈🐈	

Total number of pets brought to school = _____

OBJECTIVE: Interpret information on a picture graph.

Desmond has many toys. The picture shows Desmond's favourite toys and how many of each that he has.

Desmond's favourite toys

TOYS	NUMBER OF TOYS	TOTAL
plane		
truck		
car		
bus		
train		
soldier		

1. There are _____ toy planes.

2. Which toy is the least? How many?_____

3. There are _____ less toy trucks than toy buses.

4. There are _____more toy cars than toy trains.

5. Which toy is the most popular?_____

6. How many toys altogether does Desmond have?_____

7. Count the toys and write the numeral for each set in the total column.

THINK ABOUT IT

Children in 1C are selling tickets in a raffle. The winner of the raffle will win a cake. Whoever sells the most tickets will get a prize. The teacher of class 1C made up this chart.

Answer the questions by filling in the blank spaces.

	NAME OF PUPIL	TICKETS SOLD
1.	William	14
2.	Diedre	9
3.	Yanick	28
4.	Brandon	6
5.	Ameila	18
6.	Abby	27
7.	Peter	31
8.	Ivan	12
9.	Pedro	22
10.	Antonio	10
11.	Gabrielle	8
12.	Danielle	20
13.	Ricardo	18
14.	Shantelle	26
15.	Morris	29
16.	Theresa	13

1. Who sold the least tickets?

   _____

2. Yanick and Pedro sold _____ tickets altogether.

3. Diedre and Gabrielle together sold _____ tickets.

4. Abby and Peter together sold _____tickets.

5. Which two children sold the same amount?_____, _____

6. Who sold the most tickets?

   _____

7. Theresa should have sold _____ more tickets in order to reach Ameila's amount of tickets.

PICTOGRAMS

We can use drawings and pictures of things in a graph.
This is called a pictogram.
Example:

FAVOURITE FRUITS OF CHILDREN IN CLASS 1R

N.B.   The drawing of a fruit tells us just how many children like that particular fruit.

| Number of children | apple | papaya | pineapple | mango | orange |

1. Which fruit is liked best?_____

2. Which fruit is liked least of all?_____

3.   How many children altogether like mango and apple?_____

4. Which two fruits are liked by the same number of children?_____

5. How many children are in the class?_____

The Fraction

UNDERSTANDING FRACTIONS

The half ($\frac{1}{2}$)

This is a whole circle.

If we divide this whole circle into 2 equal parts we get 2 halves. This can be written $\frac{1}{2} + \frac{1}{2} = 1$ whole.

Two halves make one whole.

If you take a square piece of paper and fold it into 2 equal parts, each part will be half of the whole.

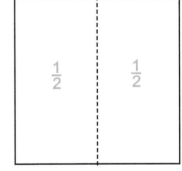

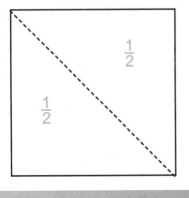

Fold the same piece of paper on the diagonal. Do you have two equal parts? Each part is one-half of the whole and is written as $\frac{1}{2}$ (one by two).

Which shapes show one half ($\frac{1}{2}$) coloured? Mark them with an X.

1.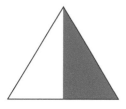

2.

3.

4.

5.

6.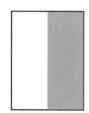

7.

8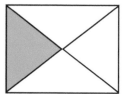

9.

10.

Look at these sets and solve them.

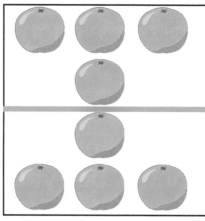
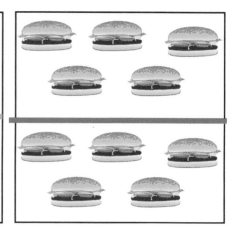

$\frac{1}{2}$ of 12 = _____ $\frac{1}{2}$ of 8 = _____ $\frac{1}{2}$ of 10 = _____

OBJECTIVE: Show $\frac{1}{2}$ of a given object or objects.

Circle a half of each set and complete the sentence.

$\frac{1}{2}$ of _____ is _____

$\frac{1}{2}$ of _____ is _____

$\frac{1}{2}$ of _____ is _____

$\frac{1}{2}$ of _____ is _____

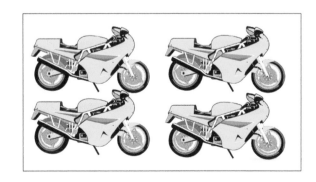

$\frac{1}{2}$ of _____ is _____

$\frac{1}{2}$ of _____ is _____

UNDERSTANDING FRACTIONS

The Quarter ($\frac{1}{4}$)

Take a sheet of square paper and fold it into four equal parts. Each of the parts is one-quarter of the paper. We write one-quarter like this $\frac{1}{4}$ (one by four).

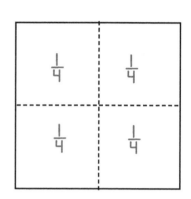

Colour a quarter ($\frac{1}{4}$) of each shape.

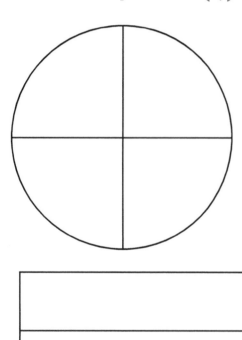

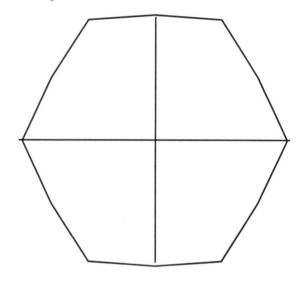

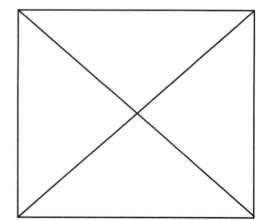

Which shapes show one-quarter ($\frac{1}{4}$)? Mark them with an X.

Circle a quarter of each set and complete the sentence.

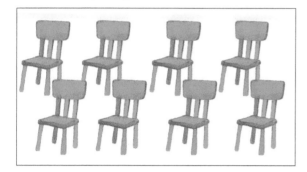

$\frac{1}{4}$ of _____ is _____

$\frac{1}{4}$ of _____ is _____

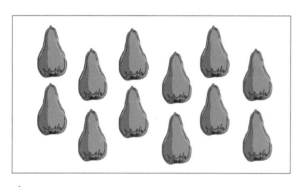

$\frac{1}{4}$ of _____ is _____

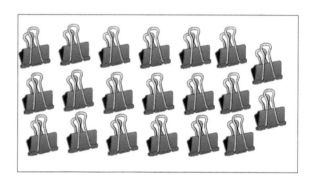

$\frac{1}{4}$ of _____ is _____

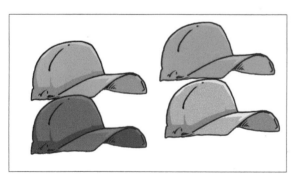

$\frac{1}{4}$ of _____ is _____

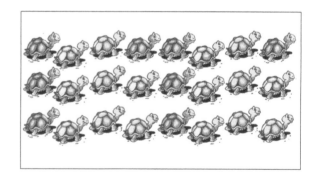

$\frac{1}{4}$ of _____ is _____

Subtraction

OBJECTIVE: Subtract whole numbers up to 2 digits.

To subtract means to take away, to minus or to find the difference.

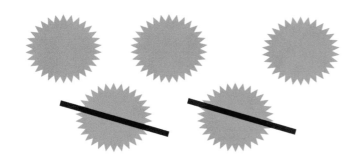

5 things take away 3 things leaves 2

$$5 - 3 = 2$$

7 take away 3 leaves 4

$$7 - 3 = \rule{2cm}{0.4pt}$$

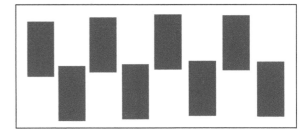

8 take away 2 leaves

$$8 - 2 = \rule{2cm}{0.4pt}$$

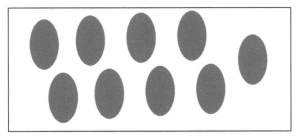

9 take away 2 leaves

$$9 - 2 = \rule{2cm}{0.4pt}$$

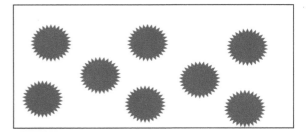

8 take away 3 leaves

$$8 - 3 = \rule{2cm}{0.4pt}$$

SUBTRACTION

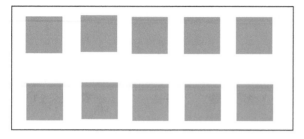

10 take away 3 leaves

10 – 3 = _____

14 take away 2 leaves

14 – 2 = _____

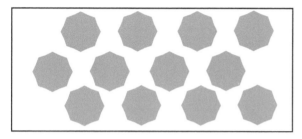

12 take away 1 leaves

12 – 1 = _____

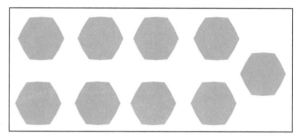

9 take away 4 leaves

9 – 4 = _____

15 take away 3 leaves

15 – 3 = _____

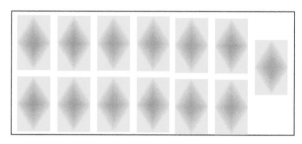

13 take away 2 leaves

13 – 2 = _____

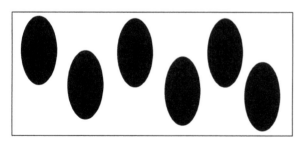

6 take away 1 leaves

6 – 1 = _____

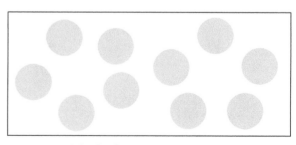

10 take away 4 leaves

10 – 4 = _____

Activity:

Write the correct answer in the boxes.

How many bikes? _____

$9 - 4 =$ ☐

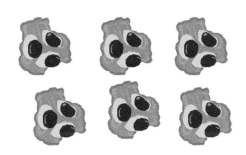

How many ackees ? _____

$6 - 3 =$ ☐

How many butterflies ? _____

$8 - 2 =$ ☐

How many fish ? _____

$10 - 3 =$ ☐

How many butterflies ? _____

$12 - 2 =$ ☐

12 - 3 = _____

7 - 6 = _____

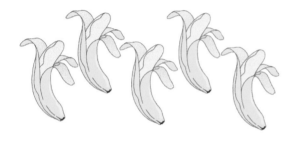

5 - 5 = _____

14 - 2 = _____

10 - 9 = _____

6 - 6 = _____

15 - 3 = _____

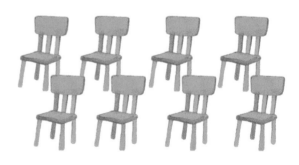

8 - 2 = _____

Using the number line 0 – 20 to show subtraction.

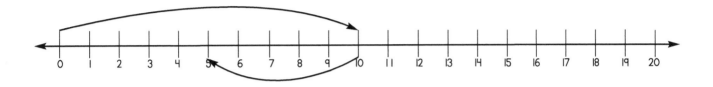

Example: 10 – 5 = ?

1.   Start at 0 and go to 10.

2.   Move backwards 5 spaces counting on in ones.

3.   We stop at 5. 10 – 5 = 5

Draw a number line 0 to 20 and do the problem below.

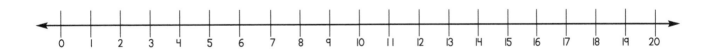

9 – 3 = _____

SUBTRACTION

Use the number line to complete the following.

1. $13 - 3 =$ _____

2. $6 - 6 =$ _____

3. $8 - 2 =$ _____

4. $12 - 3 =$ _____

5. $8 - 0 =$ _____

6. $12 - 10 =$ _____

7. $16 - 5 =$ _____

8. $13 - 0 =$ _____

Solve the following:

1. $13 - 5 =$ _____

2. $20 - 2 =$ _____

3. $18 - 4 =$ _____

4. $17 - 10 =$ _____

5. $8 - 8 =$ _____

6. $11 - 4 =$ _____

7. $15 - 4 =$ _____

8. $7 - 7 =$ _____

9. $13 - 10 =$ _____

10. $15 - 5 =$ _____

11. $12 - 4 =$ _____

12. $16 - 3 =$ _____

Give the answers to the following:

1. $8 - 1 =$ _____

6. $5 - 2 =$ _____

2. $6 - 3 =$ _____

7. $5 - 5 =$ _____

3. $9 - 2 =$ _____

8. $8 - 3 =$ _____

4. $7 - 3 =$ _____

9. $7 - 4 =$ _____

5. $10 - 2 =$ _____

10. $10 - 4 =$ _____

OBJECTIVE: Subtract zero (0) from any number.

Remember that taking away 0 (zero) from any number, the number remains the same.

For example:

$5 - 0 = 5,$ $\qquad 9 - 0 = 9,$ $\qquad 13 - 0 = 13$

Solve:

8 - 0 = ___   4 - 0 = ___   5 - 0 = ___

9 - 9 = ___   14 - 0 = ___   7 - 6 = ___

3 - 0 = ___   6 - 6 = ___   12 - 0 = ___

13 - 0 = ___   12 - 10 = ___   11 - 0 = ___

5 - 3 = ___   8 - 8 = ___   7 - 0 = ___

9 - 0 = ___   15 - 0 = ___   10 - 0 = ___

1 - 0 = ___   13 - 12 = ___   16 - 0 = ___

5 - 5 = ___   7 - 4 = ___   14 - 14 = ___

55 - ☐ = 23   ☐ - 33 = 21   89 - 45 = ☐

☐ - 33 = 10   88 - 25 = ☐   56 - 11 = ☐

70 - ☐ = 27   39 - 27 = ☐   41 - ☐ = 8

44 - ☐ = 13   54 - 20 = ☐   98 - 55 = ☐

Solve:

14	9	17	8
− 3	− 3	− 3	− 3
___	___	___	___

10	6	10	8
− 0	− 0	− 2	− 0
___	___	___	___

14	16	15	12
− 4	− 3	− 2	− 1
___	___	___	___

SUBTRACTION: TAKE AWAY

1. Miranda has 8 erasers. She lends out 3 erasers.

   Miranda has 5 erasers left.

   We say 8 take away 3 is 5.

   We write it this way 8 – 3 = 5

2. Mom gave me 6 ripe bananas. I ate 2 of the bananas.

   I have 4 bananas left.

   6 take away 2 is 4.

   6 – 2 = 4

Take away, – (minus) and find the difference, all mean the same thing, SUBTRACT.

How many letters are there in the word SUBTRACT?

Take away the first 3 letters. _____

What do you have left? _____

Find this word in your dictionary. What does it mean?

_____

SUBTRACTION: FINDING THE DIFFERENCE

Example:

John has 4 apples.

Mary has 2 apples.

John has _____ more apples than Mary.

The difference between 4 and 2 equals 2.

$$4 - 2 = 2$$

Now do these.

1. **Margaret has 9 erasers. She gave Peter 3 erasers.**
    Margaret has _____ more erasers than Peter.
    The difference between 9 and 3 equals____.

    9 − 3 = _____

2. **Themba has 10 marbles. He gave Jona 4 marbles.**
    Themba has _____ more marbles than Jona.
    The difference between 10 and 4 equals____.

    10 − 4 = _____

OBJECTIVE: Subtract two-digit number with regrouping.

SUBTRACTION OF 2-DIGIT NUMBERS WITH REGROUPING

Pay particular attention to the example.

Begin the subtraction from the ones column. 5 cannot be subtracted from 3.

T	O
$^6\cancel{7}$	3
− 3	5

Take one ten from the 7 tens of the tens column, leaving 6 tens.

T	O
$^6\cancel{7}$	$^{10+}3$
− 3	5
	8

Put this one ten above the 3 of the ones column. Add the 10 and the 3 to get 13.

Bring down the 8 to the answer line.

T	O
$^6\cancel{7}$	$^{10+}3$
− 3	5
3	8

Continue the subtraction as you would usually do.

Activity:

1.
8	3
− 3	6

2.
6	0
− 1	4

3.
6	8
− 2	9

4.
9	4
− 4	6

5.
9	1
− 3	7

6.
8	4
− 2	5

7.
7	7
− 3	8

8.
7	5
− 2	7

9. Of 87 mangoes picked on my Uncle's farm, 39 were not good. How many were good? _____

10. Kevin walked about 93 metres. My friend, John, walked 76 metres. How much further did Kevin walk? _____

11. Daniel collected 56 marbles. How many more does he need to have 88? _____

12. What is the difference between 92 and 64? _____

SUBTRACTION - TENS AND ONES

1. 25 - 13 = ?

Tens	Ones
2	5
- 1	3
1	2

Answer = 12

2. 87 - 53 = ?

Tens	Ones
8	7
- 5	3

Answer = _____

3. 60 - 37 = ?

Tens	Ones
6	9
- 3	7

Answer = _____

4. 80 - 20 = ?

Tens	Ones
8	0
- 2	0

Answer = _____

5. 36 - 23 = ?

Tens	Ones
3	6
- 2	3

Answer = _____

6. 92 - 71 = ?

Tens	Ones
9	2
- 7	1

Answer = _____

USING THE SUBTRACTION OR TAKE AWAY SIGN

When we subtract we remove or take away objects from a set. Let us subtract.

8 - 2 = _____

12 - 3 = _____

10 - 4 = _____

14 - 4 = _____

6 - 1 = _____

20 - 10 = _____

7 - 3 = _____

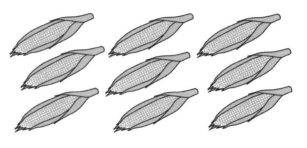

9 - 4 = _____

NUMERALS AND THEIR NUMBER NAMES 70 -100

Match number names to their numerals.

53	**fifty-five**
97	eighty-nine
89	seventy
55	**fifty-three**
68	eighty-one
60	**sixty-six**
70	ninety-seven
66	sixty-eight
81	sixty

NUMERALS AND THEIR NUMBER NAMES

Trace the numbers from 1 to 100.

1	2	3	4	5	6	7	8	9	10
11	12	13	14	15	16	17	18	19	20
21	22	23	24	25	26	27	28	29	30
31	32	33	34	35	36	37	38	39	40
41	42	43	44	45	46	47	48	49	50
51	52	53	54	55	56	57	58	59	60
61	62	63	64	65	66	67	68	69	70
71	72	73	74	75	76	77	78	79	80
81	82	83	84	85	86	87	88	89	90
91	92	93	94	95	96	97	98	99	100

There are 20 marbles and 5 plates.

Draw the marbles in the plates so that each plate has an equal number of marbles.

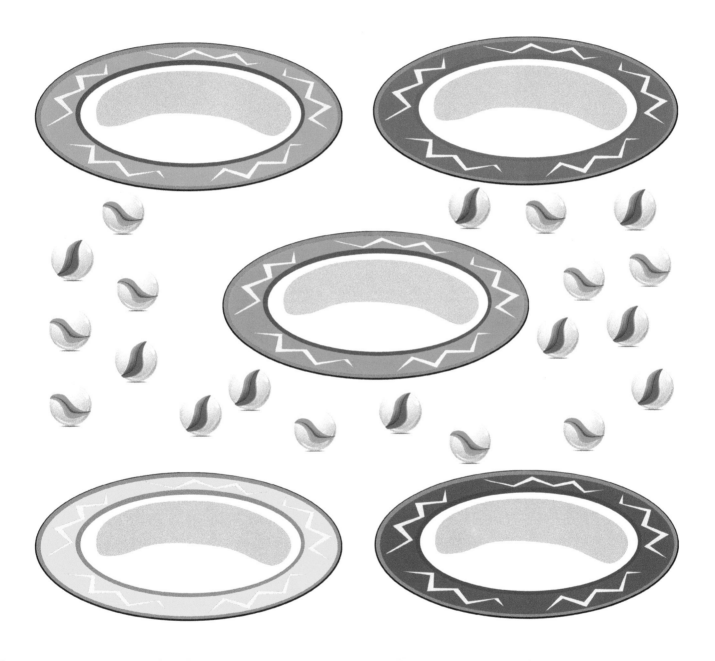

There are _____ marbles on each plate.

Look at our Jamaican money.

Coins:

Notes:

OBJECTIVE: Know the value of each coin and note.

Jamaica has many different kinds of money.
There are notes (paper money) and coins.

The coins have the faces of some of our National
Heroes on them.

Paul Bogle 10¢   Marcus Garvey 25¢   Alexander Bustamante $1

Norman Manley $5   George William Gordon $10   Marcus Garvey $20

Jamaican Coins

Sam Sharpe $50   Donald Sangster $100   Nanny of the Maroons $500

Michael Manley $1000   Hugh Shearer $5000

Jamaican notes

$ This is the dollar sign.   **¢ This is the cent sign.**

One hundred cents (100¢) make one dollar ($1)

Example: 80¢ + 30¢ = 110¢

110¢ means $1.10

The full stop separtes the dollar from the cents.

Activity:

1. Which of these sets has the greater amount of money?

 _____    _____

2. What is the value of each money?

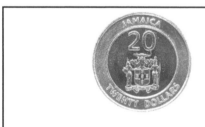	

3. Let's exchange  for coins.
Name the coins.

_____

4. How many  make  ? _____

5. How much money is?

   _____

6. What is my change?

MY BILL	I GIVE	MY CHANGE
80¢	$1	
70¢	25¢ 25¢ 25¢	
90¢	$1	
50¢	30¢ 20¢ 20¢	

Activity:

Answer the following questions about Jamaican money.

1. Who is the hero or heroine on the

    a. 25¢ coin _____

    b. $500 note _____

    c. $20 coin _____

    d. $50 coin _____

    e. $10 coin _____

    f. $1,000 note _____

    g. $100 note _____

2. Which notes do not have pictures of Jamaican heroes?

    _____

3. Is the picture of the person on the $500 note a Jamaican hero/heroine?

    _____

4. What was the hero on the $50 note famous for?

    _____

5. Was the picture of the person on the $100 note a Prime Minister or a hero?

    _____

ADDITION

Add the following:

$	¢
6 .	14
+ 3 .	05

$	¢
8 .	6
+ 1 .	3

$	¢
5 .	5
+ 5 .	3

$	¢
5 .	6
+ 4 .	2

$	¢
2 .	21
+ 7 .	32

$	¢
13 .	9
+ 22 .	0

$	¢
8 .	12
+ 2 .	16

$	¢
7 .	05
+ 3 .	12

$	¢
9 .	07
+ 4 .	02

How many cents in all?

a. 5¢ + 4¢ = _____   g. 4¢ + 7¢ = _____   m. 7¢ + 2¢ = _____

b. 9¢ + 2¢ = _____   h. 10¢ + 2¢ = _____   n. 3¢ + 3¢ = _____

c. 4¢ + 6¢ = _____   i. 4¢ + 8¢ = _____   o. 8¢ + 5¢ = _____

d. 3¢ + 4¢ = _____   j. 5¢ + 2¢ = _____   p. 2¢ + 3¢ = _____

e. 10¢ + 1¢ = _____   k. 8¢ + 1¢ = _____

f. 3¢ + 2¢ = _____   l. 7¢ + 5¢ = _____

OBJECTIVE: Add and subtract money.

SUBTRACTION

Solve:

	$	¢
	8 .	22
−	3 .	01

	$	¢
	6 .	68
−	1 .	40

	$	¢
	9 .	15
−	5 .	03

	$	¢
	9 .	56
−	2 .	23

	$	¢
	7 .	54
−	0 .	21

	$	¢
	9 .	75
−	3 .	14

	$	¢
	7 .	63
−	4 .	21

	$	¢
	8 .	35
−	2 .	14

	$	¢
	5 .	40
−	4 .	10

	$	¢
	7 .	24
−	3 .	13

	$	¢
	9 .	46
−	3 .	14

	$	¢
	6 .	15
−	2 .	13

OBJECTIVE: Solve worded problems using money.

Our school is having its annual Fair. These food items are being sold at the food tent.

MENU

Fried Chicken & Roll	$90.00	Ham Sandwich	$60.00
Cheese Burger	$60.00	Cheese sandwich	$40.00
Hot Dog	$50.00	Corned Beef Sandwich	$40.00
Hamburger	$80.00	Orange Juice	$30.00
Bun/Cheese	$40.00	Coconut Water	$30.00
Patty	$50.00	Pineapple Juice	$30.00

1. Which item costs the most? _____

2. If I want a bun and cheese, what is the cost? _____

3. How much will I pay for 1 hot dog? _____

4. What is the cost of 1 patty and an orange juice? _____

5. I like corned beef sandwiches. How much will I pay for two corned beef sandwiches? _____

6. 1 ham sandwich and 1 pineapple juice cost? _____

7. 1 hamburger and 1 coconut water cost? _____

8. Which item costs the least? _____

9. Of the three sandwiches on the Menu, which is the most expensive? _____

10. Mark, Jonas and Peter bought 3 patties. How much did the 3 patties cost altogether? _____

OBJECTIVE: Establish equal values of different combination of notes and coins.

SHOPPING

Exercise book $50   Eraser $12   Pencil $15   Pen $40   Apple $30

a. One pencil costs $_____. How many pencils can I buy

with $60? _____

b. An exercise book costs $ _____. How many exercise books

can I buy with $100? _____

c. What is the cost of 3 pencils and 2 exercise books? _____

d. How many erasers can I buy with $36? _____

e. David wants to buy 1 apple, 2 pencils and 2 exercise books. How

much will he have to spend?_____

f. Three apples cost $_____.

Apple $20   Ruler $20   Ball $30   Slice of cake $30

Hamburger $60   Pencil   60¢   Banana $4.00   Sweet Candy 50c

Bar of Chocolate $70   glass of orange juice $50

How much must I pay if I buy …?

a.   2 sweets _____

b.   I hamburger _____

c.   2 apples _____

d.   I slice of cake and I apple _____

e.   I bar of chocolate and I ruler _____

f.   I slice of cake and I glass of orange juice _____

Karen would like to play with Kevin.

a. Karen: I hid three coins. They make up $30.00.

What coins did I hide?

Kevin: _____

_____

b. Karen: I hid one note and two coins. They make up $70.00.

What note and coins did I hide?

_____

_____

c. Nicola bought a computer game for $15.

Ken bought the same game for $8.

How much more than Ken did Nicola pay for the game?

_____

_____

d. A T-shirt costs $6. A pair of socks costs $5.

What is the cost of the T-shirt and the pair of socks altogether?

_____

_____

Are We Odd or Even?

LET US READ: WHAT IS AN EVEN NUMBER?

An even number is a number that can be shared into two (2) equal sets exactly without leaving anything.

I can share the 2 footballs into 2 equal sets. Nothing is left over.

I can share the 6 footballs into 2 equal sets. Nothing is left over.

I can share the 8 footballs into 2 equal sets. Nothing is left over.

The even numbers less than 10 are:

0, 2, 4, 6, and 8

Any number ending in 0, 2, 4, 6, or 8 is an even number.

Which of these sets contains an even number of objects?
Circle the answer.

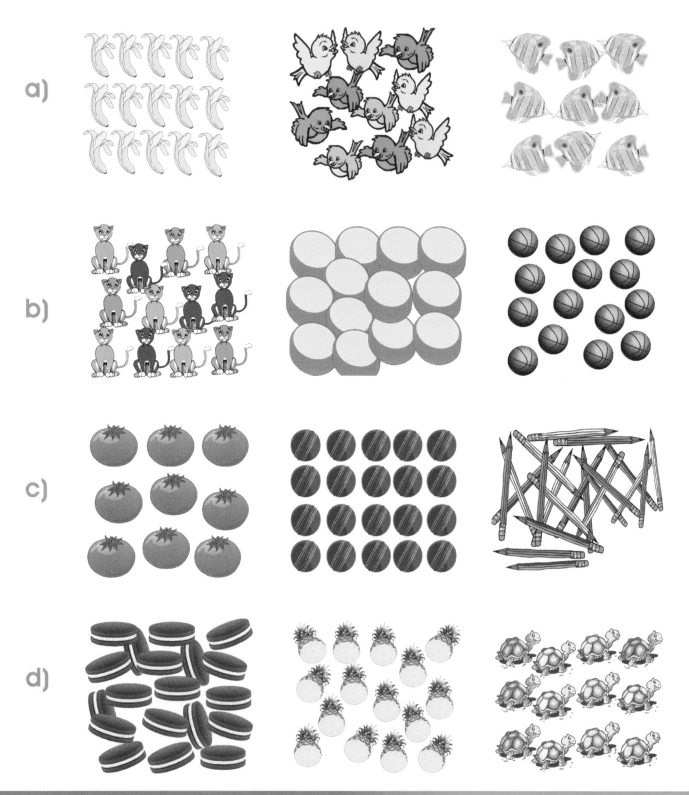

a)

b)

c)

d)

OBJECTIVE: Know that even numbers have the digit 0, 2, 4, 6 or 8 in its ones place.

Here are some even numbers. Study them.
Even numbers usually end with 0, 2, 4, 6, or 8.

● ●	2 two	● ● ● ● ● ● ● ● ● ● ● ●	12 twelve
● ● ● ●	4 four	● ● ● ● ● ● ● ● ● ● ● ● ● ●	14 fourteen
● ● ● ● ● ●	6 six	● ● ● ● ● ● ● ● ● ● ● ● ● ● ● ●	16 sixteen
● ● ● ● ● ● ● ●	8 eight	● ● ● ● ● ● ● ● ● ● ● ● ● ● ● ● ● ●	18 eighteen
● ● ● ● ● ● ● ● ● ●	10 ten	● ● ● ● ● ● ● ● ● ● ● ● ● ● ● ● ● ● ● ●	20 twenty

Answer the following questions by circling the correct answer. The first one is done for you.

a) Is three an even number?   Yes   (No)

b) Is four an even number?   Yes   No

c) Is eighteen an even number?   Yes   No

ARE WE ODD OR EVEN?

Circle the even numbers from the following. What is the pattern? The first even number is circled for you.

1	(2)	3	4	5	6	7
8	9	10	11	12	13	14
15	16	17	18	19	20	

Answer the following questions by circling the correct answer. The first one is done for you.

a) Is sixteen an even number?   (Yes)   no

b) Is eleven an even number?   Yes   no

c) Is ten an even number?   Yes   no

d) Write all the even numbers from one to twenty.

_____

EVEN NUMBERS / COUNTING BY TWOS

Circle the even numbers.

1	2	3	4	5
6	7	8	9	10
11	12	13	14	15
16	17	18	19	20
21	22	23	24	25
26	27	28	29	30
31	32	33	34	35
36	37	38	39	40
41	42	43	44	45
46	47	48	49	50

ODD NUMBERS

OBJECTIVE: Know that odd numbers have the digit 1, 3, 5, 7 or 9 in its ones place.

Odd numbers are numbers that cannot be divided by two exactly.

Here are some odd numbers. Study them. Odd numbers usually end with 1, 3, 5, 7 or 9.

●	1 one	●●●●● ●●●●●	11 eleven
●●●	3 three	●●●●●●● ●●●●●●	13 thirteen
●●●●●	5 five	●●●●●●●● ●●●●●●●	15 fifteen
●●●● ●●●	7 seven	●●●●●●●●● ●●●●●●●●	17 seventeen
●●●●● ●●●●	9 nine	●●●●●●●●●● ●●●●●●●●●	19 nineteen

Answer the following questions by circling the correct answer. The first one is done for you.

a) Is twelve an odd number?   Yes   (No)

b) Is eleven an odd number?   Yes   No

c) Is one an odd number?   Yes   No

OBJECTIVE: Know the difference between odd and even.

Count the objects in each set and put the answer in the box. Is the number odd or even? Circle the correct answer.

Number of books

=

Number is odd / even

Number of eggs

=

Number is odd / even

Number of caps

=

Number is odd / even

Number of footballs

=

Number is odd / even

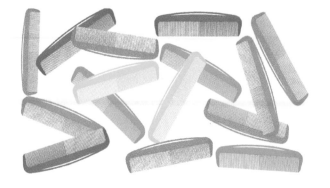

Number of combs

= ☐

Number is odd / even

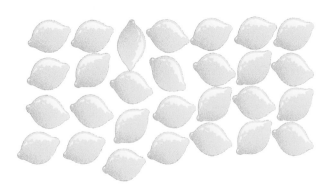

Number of lemons

= ☐

Number is odd / even

Circle the even numbers and X the odd numbers.

12	13	14	15	16	17	18	19	20	21
22	23	24	25	26	27	28	29	30	31
32	33	34	35	36	37	38	39	40	41

Activity:

LET US READ

Read the passage below and answer the questions that follow.

On Saturday my mother and I went to the market. First, she bought six fingers of bananas from a very nice vendor named Betty. Bananas were not the only food items Betty had selling. She also had yam, mangoes, apples and plantains. Mom bought apples. My brother and I love apples. In total, my mother bought nine apples because six apples were too little to feed my brother and me. Mom bought many items. It was a long day. We walked for a very long time. My mother could not find the last item on the list. Oranges were scarce. At last she found a vendor selling oranges. My mother wanted twenty-four oranges but the vendor only had nineteen left. My mother bought them all. I love going to the market with my mother. We get to see a lot of food items.

a. How many fingers of bananas did mother buy? _____

b. Was it an odd number of bananas? _____

c. How many apples did mother buy? _____

d. How many oranges did mother buy? _____

e. Were an odd number of apples bought? _____

f. Did mother buy an odd number of oranges? _____

Tens and Ones

COUNT IN TENS

1	2	3	4	5	6	7	8	9	10
11	12	13	14	15	16	17	18	19	20
21	22	23	24	25	26	27	28	29	30
31	32	33	34	35	36	37	38	39	40
41	42	43	44	45	46	47	48	49	50
51	52	53	54	55	56	57	58	59	60
61	62	63	64	65	66	67	68	69	70
71	72	73	74	75	76	77	78	79	80
81	82	83	84	85	86	87	88	89	90
91	92	93	94	95	96	97	98	99	100

Activity:

Fill in the numbers that are missing.

10		30		50		70		90	
	20		40		60		80		100

GROUPS OF TENS

Count

10 + 1	○○○○○ ○○○○○	+	○	11 Eleven
10 + 2	○○○○○ ○○○○○	+	○ ○	12 Twelve
10 + 3	○○○○○ ○○○○○	+	○ ○ ○	13 Thirteen
10 + 4	○○○○○ ○○○○○	+	○ ○ ○ ○	14 Fourteen
10 + 5	○○○○○ ○○○○○	+	○ ○ ○ ○ ○	15 Fifteen
10 + 6	○○○○○ ○○○○○	+	○○○○○ ○	16 Sixteen
10 + 7	○○○○○ ○○○○○	+	○○○○○ ○ ○	17 Seventeen
10 + 8	○○○○○ ○○○○○	+	○○○○○ ○ ○ ○	18 Eighteen
10 + 9	○○○○○ ○○○○○	+	○○○○○ ○○○○	19 Nineteen
10 + 10	○○○○○ ○○○○○	+	○○○○○ ○○○○○	20 Twenty
10 + 11	○○○○○ ○○○○○	+	○○○○○○ ○○○○○	21 Twenty-one
10 + 12	○○○○○ ○○○○○	+	○○○○○○ ○○○○○○	22 Twenty-two
10 + 13	○○○○○ ○○○○○	+	○○○○○○○ ○○○○○○	23 Twenty-three

TENS AND ONES

How many tens and ones?

10 + 10 + 2

_____ tens + _____ ones

= _____

10 + 10 + 10 + 10 + 3

_____ tens + _____ ones

= _____

10 + 8

_____ tens + _____ ones

= _____

10 + 10 + 10 + 10 + 10

_____ tens + _____ ones

= _____

10 + 10 + 10 + 10

_____ tens + _____ ones

= _____

10 + 10 + 10 + 10 + 5

_____ tens + _____ ones

= _____

10 + 10 + 10

_____ tens + _____ ones

= _____

10 + 10 + 4

_____ tens + _____ ones

= _____

10 + 10 + 10 + 8

_____ tens + _____ ones

= _____

10 + 10 + 10 + 7

_____ tens + _____ ones

= _____

Counting, Use Counters

1. **Count the sticks.**

10 sticks = 1 ten

20 sticks = 2 tens

= ten

= twenty

2. Count the bundles of 10

10,   20,   30, 40, 50

5 tens ... 50 ... fifty

6 tens ... 60 ... sixty

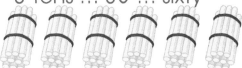

7 tens ... 70 ... seventy

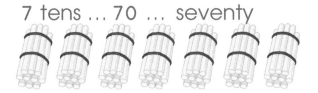

8 tens ... 80 ... eighty

9 tens ... 90 ... ninety

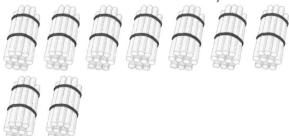

10 tens ... 100 ... hundred

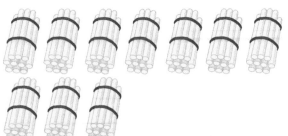

3. Now let us count on in tens and ones.

2 **more**   2 **less**

40 41 42 43 44 45 46 47 48 49 50

Count on from 42.   Count backwards from 50.

44 is 2 more than 42.   48 is 2 less than 50.

44 is greater than 42.   48 is smaller than 50.

4. Which number is greater?
    Which number is smaller?

    68   73

    7 tens is greater than 6 tens.
    Therefore, 73 is greater than 68
    68 is smaller than 73 .

5. Which number is greater?
    Which number is smaller?

    78   75

    Are the tens equal?
    Are the ones equal?

    ☐ tens is greater than ☐ tens.
    Therefore, ☐ is greater than ☐
    ☐ is smaller than ☐ .

6. Compare 58, 74 and 86.

    58   74   86

Which is the smallest number? ☐
Which is the greatest number? ☐
Why is it the smallest?   _____
Why is 86 greater than 74?   _____

Circle the sets of 10 and write the numbers. The first one is done for you.

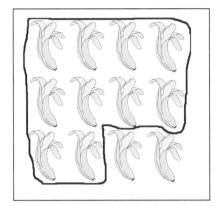

Tens	Ones
1	2

Tens	Ones

Tens	Ones

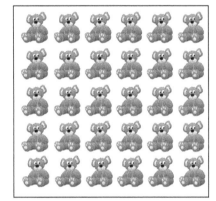

Tens	Ones

Tens	Ones

Tens	Ones

Tens	Ones

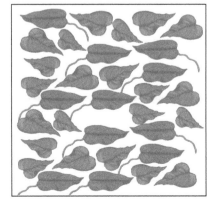

Tens	Ones

TENS AND ONES

How many tens and ones?

1. 24 = _____ tens _____ ones

2. 17 = _____ tens _____ ones

3. 22 = _____ tens _____ ones

4. 25 = _____ tens _____ ones

5. 19 = _____ tens _____ ones

6. 36 = _____ tens _____ ones

7. 20 = _____ tens _____ ones

8. 21 = _____ tens _____ ones

9. 43 = _____ tens _____ ones

10. 31 = _____ tens _____ ones

Write the numerals for each.

1. 1 ten and 7 ones = _____

2. 5 tens and 9 ones = _____

3. 7 ones and 5 tens = _____

4. 5 ones and 2 tens = _____

5. 6 tens and 5 ones = _____

6. 4 tens and 3 ones = _____

7. 8 tens and 5 ones = _____

8. 4 tens and 7 ones = _____

9. 8 ones and 6 tens = _____

10. 9 ones and 7 tens = _____

TENS AND ONES: ADDITION

We always add the ones column first when we are adding numbers having 2 digits, then we add the tens column.

	Tens	Ones
	5	3
+	1	3
	6	6

Answer = 66

	Tens	Ones
	7	3
+	1	2

Answer = _____

	Tens	Ones
	7	1
+	2	2
	9	3

Answer = 93

	Tens	Ones
	4	4
+	3	2

Answer = _____

	Tens	Ones
	9	2
+	1	4

Answer = _____

	Tens	Ones
	9	2
+	1	4

Answer = _____

Remember to add the Ones column first, then the Tens column.

Add the following:

30 + 50

Tens	Ones
3	0
+ 5	0

Answer

82 + 25

Tens	Ones
8	2
+ 2	5

Answer

48 + 10

Tens	Ones
4	8
+ 1	0

Answer

61 + 25

Tens	Ones
6	1
+ 2	5

Answer

14 + 15

Tens	Ones
1	4
+ 1	5

Answer

72 + 26

Tens	Ones
7	2
+ 2	6

Answer

23 + 50

Tens	Ones
2	3
+ 5	0

Answer

18 + 70

Tens	Ones
1	8
+ 7	0

Answer

Place Value

1.

10   3

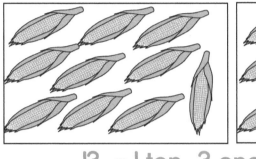

Tens	Ones
1	3

13 = 1 ten 3 ones

2.

10   8

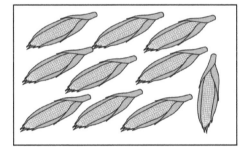

Tens	Ones

18 = _____ten _____ones

3.

10   6

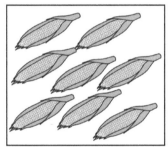

Tens	Ones

16 = _____ten _____ones

Group the following numbers in their proper places.

17

Tens	Ones

20

Tens	Ones

28

Tens	Ones

30

Tens	Ones

25

Tens	Ones

43

Tens	Ones

22

Tens	Ones

44

Tens	Ones

34

Tens	Ones

36

Tens	Ones

56

Tens	Ones

18

Tens	Ones

16

Tens	Ones

13

Tens	Ones

Circle the number which is greater.

1.   18   20   **By how much greater** _____.

2.   12   11   **By how much greater** _____.

3.   23   20   **By how much greater** _____.

4.   15   17   **By how much greater** _____.

5.   14   21   **By how much greater** _____.

Circle the number which is less.

1.   12   9   **By how much less** _____.

2.   13   14   **By how much less** _____.

3.   18   20   **By how much less** _____.

4.   9   8   **By how much less** _____.

5.   13   16   **By how much less** _____.

Multiplication

OBJECTIVE: Use repeated addtion to find the product of a set of numbers.

ADDING THE SAME NUMBER

Look at the pictures. Fill in the boxes.

2 + 2 + 2 + 2 = 8

 4 twos = 8

There are 8 fish together.

3 + 3 + 3 + 3 + 3 = 15

5 threes = 15

There are ☐ birds altogether.

COMPLETE.

☐ + ☐ + ☐ = ☐

☐ fours = ☐

There are ☐ turtles altogether.

There are 3 bowls. Draw 3 marbles in each bowl.

3 threes = _____.   There are _____ marbles altogether.

There are 4 bowls. Draw 5 marbles in each bowl.

4 _____ = _____.   There are _____ marbles altogether.

MULTIPLICATION STORIES

Look, count and write.

a)   There are _____ groups of birds. Each group has _____ birds.

2 + 2 + 2 + 2 = _____. There are _____ birds altogether.

b)   There are _____ groups of turtles. Each group has _____ turtles.

___ + ___ + ___ = ___.   There are _____ turtles altogether.

c)   There are _____ groups of burgers. Each group has _____ burgers.

___ + ___ + ___ + ___ = ___.

There are _____burgers altogether.

What are the next three numbers?

11, 12, 13, ___, ___, ___

Find the missing numbers in the following number patterns.

1. (19) (16) (13) ( ) ( ) ( )

2. (8) ( ) (12) (14) ( ) ( )

3. (18) ( ) ( ) ( ) (6) (3)

4. (13) (14) ( ) ( ) (17) ( )

Arrange the numbers in order. Begin with the greatest number

| 12 | | 16 |
| 18 | 20 | 13 |

___, ___, ___, ___, ___

WHAT IS 1 MORE?

What is one more than 14?

14

15

1 more than 14 is 15

Do these: What is...

1. I more than 17? ____
2. I more than 18? ____
3. I more than 20? ____

4. 4 more than 90? ____
5. 2 more than 20? ____
6. 5 more than 80? ____

Answer the following questions. What is...

1. I less than 12? ____
2. 3 more than 18?
3. 2 less than 18?

4. 7 less than 100? ____
5. 3 less than 65? ____
6. 5 less than 51? ____

7. Arrange these numbers in order beginning with the smallest.

13   19   20   16   9   ____, ____, ____, ____, ____.

8. Complete the number pattern.
   48,   44,   40,   ____,   ____,   28.

9. Use a tool on the computer to make any pattern using two shapes. Point to the pattern. Ask your classmates what comes next. You should use only two attributes (shape, size, colour).

Possible patterns:

Change in shape, size, and colour

Change in shape and colour

Change in shape and size.

CLOSED PATHS

What is a simple closed path?

A closed path begins and ends at the same point. It does not cross over itself.

Example:

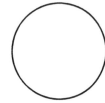 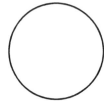

Circle the simple closed path in each box.

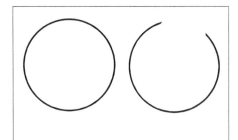 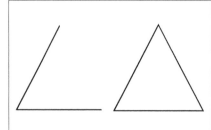 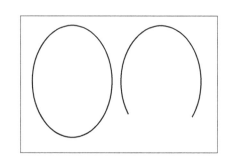

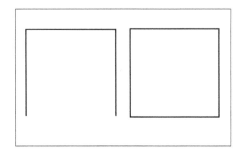 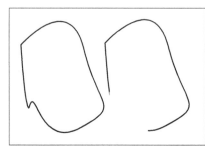 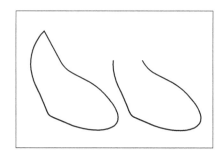

WHAT IS A SOLID?

A solid shape has many surfaces. Solids are of all shapes and sizes and they take up room and so they have volume. Some shapes even have curved faces.

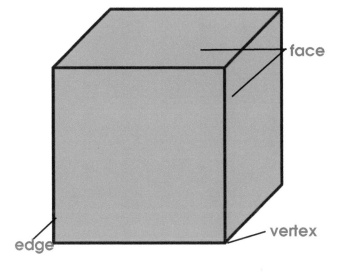

face

vertex

edge

The flat surface of a solid is its **face**.

The line formed when two faces meet is called an **edge** of a solid.

The point where three or more edges meet is a corner of a solid or its **vertex (plural – vertices)**.

The solid figures with faces, vertices and edges are the cube, cuboid, prism and pyramid.

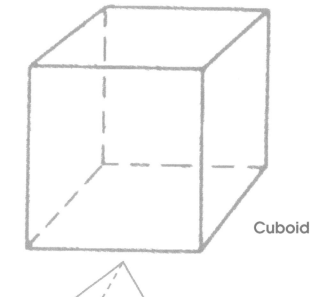

Cuboid

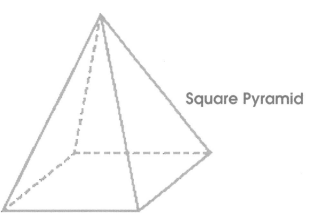

Square Pyramid

Triangle prism

3- Dimensional figures with curved surfaces.

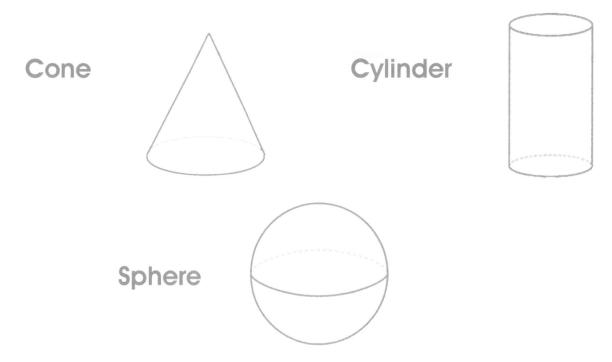

Cone

Cylinder

Sphere

Activity:

Look around your class and at home and draw 3 figures for each of these shapes.

FINDING THE UNKNOWN

OBJECTIVE: Find the number that the symbol represents to make the mathematical sentence true.

Examples:

a. If $x = 3$

Then $x + x =$
$\quad 3 + 3 = 6$

b. If $x = 2$

Then $x + x + x =$
$\quad 2 + 2 + 2 = 6$

c. If N = 3. What is N + 2?

$\quad$ N + 2 = 3 + 2
$\quad$ 3 + 2 = 5

d. If $x = 4$. What is $x + x + x$?

$\quad x + x + x = 4 + 4 + 4$
$\quad 4 + 4 + 4 + 12$

Do these.

1. n = 2. What is n + 6?

$\quad$ n + 6 = ☐ + 6

$\quad$ ☐ + 6

2. If n = 5. What is n + 5?

$\quad$ n + 5 = ☐ + 5

$\quad$ ☐ + 5

3. If ☐ = 4.

Then ☐ + ☐ + 2 = ____

4. If $x = 6$. What is $x + x + x$?

$\quad$ ☐ + ☐ + ☐ = ____

5. If $\triangle = 12$
$\quad$ Then $\triangle - 4$

$\quad$ = _____

6. $\triangle = 6$
$\quad$ Then $\triangle - 3$

$\quad$ = _____

7. $\triangle = 10$
$\quad$ Then $\triangle - 5$

$\quad$ = _____

FINDING THE UNKNOWN

Examples:

a. $4 - \triangle = 2$
   $(4 - 2 = 2)$

b. $6 - \triangle = 3$
   $(6 - 3 = 3)$

Now do these.

SUBTRACTION

$7 - \boxed{} = 3$

$8 - \boxed{} = 3$

$\boxed{} - 10 = 2$

$9 - \boxed{} = 6$

$10 - \boxed{} = 5$

$18 - \boxed{} = 9$

$20 - \boxed{} = 15$

ADDITION

$6 + \boxed{} = 8$

$8 + \boxed{} = 10$

$4 + \boxed{} = 8$

$\boxed{} + 7 = 10$

$85 + \boxed{} = 100$

$15 + \boxed{} = 25$

$27 + 6 = \boxed{}$

$42 + 48 = \boxed{}$

$38 + 6 = \boxed{}$

Probability

We can describe events or things using these words:
certain   maybe   impossible

Select the correct answer to the following questions.

1. If you select a cap without looking, how likely is it that you will pick a red one?

certain   **maybe**   impossible

3. If you select a butterfly without looking, how likely is it that you will pick a yellow one?

certain   **maybe**   impossible

2. How likely is it that the spinner will land on a green space?

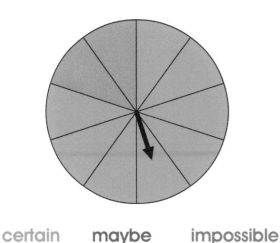

certain   **maybe**   impossible

4. How likely is it that the spinner will land on a blue space?

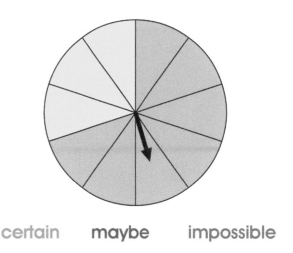

certain   **maybe**   impossible

255

PROBABILITY

5. If you select a butterfly without looking, how likely is it that you will pick a yellow one?

certain **maybe** impossible

8. If you select a butterfly without looking, how likely is it that you will pick a green one?

certain **maybe** impossible

6. How likely is it that the spinner will land on a red space?

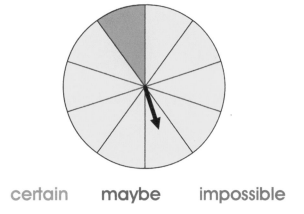

certain **maybe** impossible

9. If you select a fruit without looking, how likely is it that you will pick a red one?

certain **maybe** impossible

7. How likely is it that the spinner will land on a blue space?

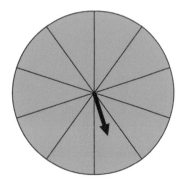

certain **maybe** impossible

10. How likely is it that the spinner will land on a red space?

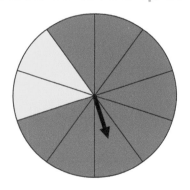

certain **maybe** impossible

ASSESSMENT

PART 1

1. How many leaves? Write the number and the number name.

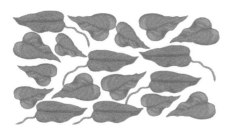

_____   _____

2. How many Tens and Ones are there in 38?

_____ Tens   _____ Ones

3. Circle the number which is greater.

24   42

4. Add the following:
$$\begin{array}{r} 38 \\ + \ 48 \\ \hline \end{array}$$

5. John has 9 apples. James has 6 apples. How many apples do they have in all? _____

6. Danielle has 56 cents. She gave away 4 cents. She now has _____ cents left.

7. Circle $\frac{1}{2}$ of the set below.

8. Draw six more circles. Write the total number of circles in the box.

○ ○ ○ ○ ○ ○
○ ○ ○ ○ ○ ○
○ ○ ○ ○ ○ ○

9. Circle groups of Ten. Write how many there are.

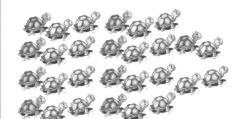

Tens	Ones

10. Circle the number name for 18.

Eight   Eighteen   Eighty

257

11. How many 2 litres of material will fill the large container?

_____

2 litres   12 litres

12. Put in the hands to show half past five.

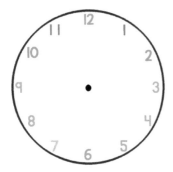

13. Circle the correct answer

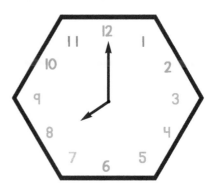

nine o'clock   seven o'clock

eight o'clock

14. Gabrielle has 25 guineps. Lisa has 12 guineps. How many more guineps has Gabrielle than Lisa?

_____

15. Circle the shapes which are exactly the same as the one in the box.

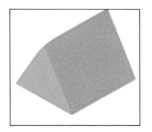

PART 2

1. What fraction is coloured?

_____

2. Measure the lines using a centimetre ruler. Write the lengths under each line.

3. What times are shown on these clocks?

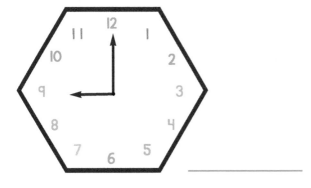

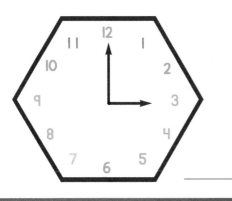

_____

4. Write the number fifty-nine in figures. _____

5. if I spend $50 for a patty, how much change must I receive from $100 (one hundred dollars)?

_____

6. Twenty-five children in a class are boys and 15 are girls. How many children are in the class?

_____

7. What is the value of the 4 in the number 49? _____

8. 61 + 34 = ☐

9. 25 – 13 = ☐

10. Write the number 56 in words.

_____

11. Look at the Pictogram. It shows the favourite ice-cream flavours of some children.

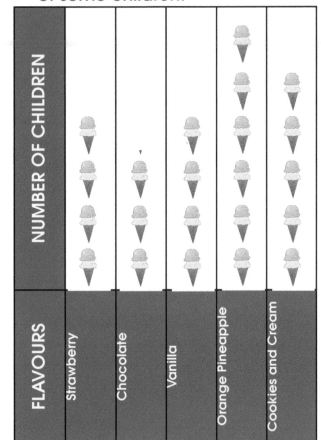

a. Which flavour is liked the least?

_____

b. Which flavour is liked the most?

_____

c. The same number of children like two flavours. Which two flavours?

_____

d. Which is the second most liked flavour? _____

e. How many children are in the class? _____

12. Name the shapes.

_____

13. What fraction is not coloured? __

14. $21 + 15 =$ ☐

15. $52 + 27 =$ ☐

16. $11 + 21 =$ ☐

17. $26 - 13 =$ ☐

18. $68 - 15 =$ ☐

19. Arrange these numbers from largest to smallest?

37, 92, 16, 51, 84, 22

____, ____, ____, ____, ____, ____

20. $40 + 15 =$ ☐

PART 3

1. Colour the parts to match each fraction written below its shape.

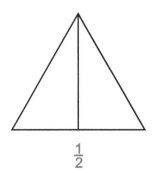

$\frac{1}{2}$

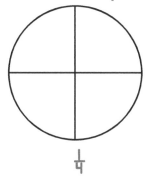

$\frac{1}{4}$

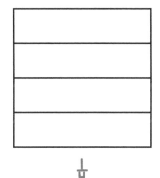

$\frac{1}{4}$

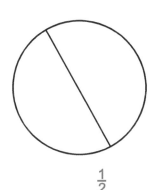

$\frac{1}{2}$

2.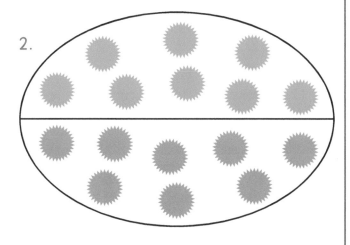

    a. How many in all? _____

    b. How many in each set? _____

3.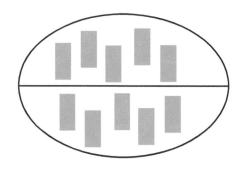

    $\frac{1}{2}$ of 10 = _____

4. 12 + 7 = _____

5. 19 − 8 = _____

6. Gavin bought 3 buns. His friend gave him 9 more buns. Gavin now has _____ buns.

7. Some boys in grade 1C were playing marbles. Josh had 12 marbles. Michael had 9 marbles. How many marbles in all did the boys have? _____

8. There were 9 mangoes on the table. Kim ate 5 of the mangoes. Tom ate 4 mangoes. How many mangoes were left? _____

9.
```
   5 5
 - 4 0
```

10.
```
   7 0
 - 2 0
```

11.
```
   6 7
 - 5 6
```

12. 41 + 6 = _____

Write the number for each of these.

13. I Ten and 7 Ones = _____

14. 7 Tens and 4 Ones = _____

15. 7 Ones and I Ten = _____

16. 30 = ____ Tens and ____ Ones

17. 46 = ____ Tens and ____ Ones

18. 64 = ____ Tens and ____ Ones

19. 55 = ____ Tens and ____ Ones

20. 83 = ____ Tens and ____ Ones

21. Which of the following is equal to 69?
    a) 54 + 15   b) 61 + 9
    c) 30 + 29

22. 5 tens 6 ones is the same as
    _____

23. Circle the two numbers that make 7 tens and 16 ones.
    42   86   44   75   67

24. Complete the number pattern.
    100, 85, 70, ____, ____, 125

25. Take away 3 tens 8 ones from 7 tens 4 ones. _____

26. Chris had $40. He spent $16 on a toy. How much had he left?
    _____

27. There were 38 pupils in the canteen. 17 were girls. How many pupils were boys? _____

28. 95 is 10 more than _____?

29. Subtract 3 from 30 = _____

30. 55 + 5 = _____

Extended Thinking

TASK 1

25 grade 1M students are going on an educational trip to Spanish Town. 10 parents will go with the students.

1.   How many people are going on the trip?   _____

Show how you know your answer is correct.

TASK 2

Look at these shapes

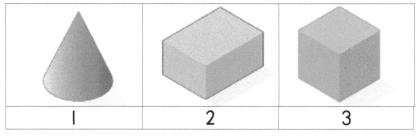

1.   How is shape 1 different from shapes 2 and 3?

_____

_____

_____

TASK 3

Find the missing part (the number that should fit in the blank space).

a) $10 + \underline{\hspace{2cm}} = 15$ b) $11 + \underline{\hspace{2cm}} = 15$

c) $18 - \underline{\hspace{2cm}} = 15$ d) $15 = \underline{\hspace{2cm}} + 9$

TASK 4

At Tiana's home the family has dogs and birds as pets.

1.   How many legs are there on one dog?   _____

2.   How many legs on 4 dogs?   _____

3.   How many legs on 5 birds?   _____

4.   On the verandah are 3 dogs and 4 birds.
     How many legs ae there altogether?   _____

Show how you know that your answer is correct.

General Instructions: Read carefully, then complete each task.

TASK 5:

This task has two parts: Part 1 has one question and Part 2 has two questions

Shopping at the Supermarket

On Saturday, your mother took you to the supermarket with her. You helped her with weighing produce and packing the groceries in the cart.

Part 1

The pictures below show some of the items your mother purchased at the supermarket and their prices.

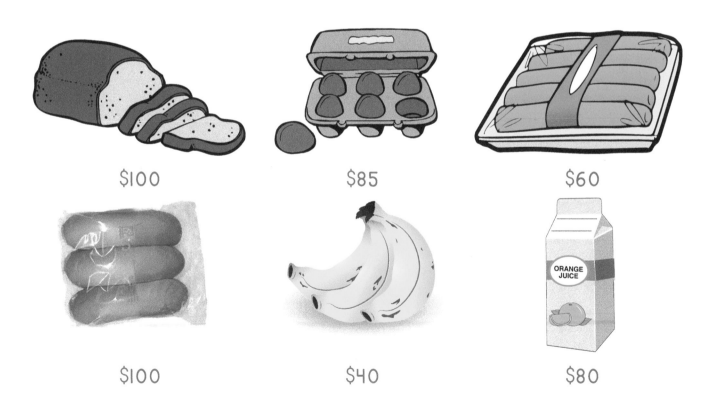

$100	$85	$60
$100	$40	$80

I. Based on the information given above place a tick (✓) to say if the statements below are **TRUE** or **FALSE**.

STATEMENT	TRUE	FALSE
The two bread mother purchased cost the same money.		
I can buy 3 orange juices with $200.		
The **cheapest** item is the hot dog sausage.		
If I want bread and eggs only, I will pay $180.		

Part 2

Mother took the following money out of her purse to pay the cashier.

I. Which National Hero/Heroine is found on the $500 note?

Circle your response below.

Marcus Garvey   **Donald Sangster**   **Nanny of the Maroons**

2. If you have four of the $50 notes, name three items you could purchase
    together from the food items in **Part 1.** In the box below **write the name or
    draw** the three items and show your calculations to prove that you can buy
    these food items.

General Instructions: Read carefully, then complete each task.

TASK 6:

This task has two parts: Part 1 has two questions and Part 2 has one question.

Visiting Grandma

It is summer holiday and you will be visiting your Grandma in another town for two weeks. You have to be on time to catch the different buses that will take you there.

Part 1

You are standing in the bus station and you saw the clock which shows the time your first bus will arrive.

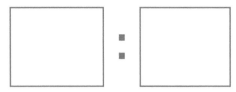

1. What time will the first bus arrive?

    ☐ **:** ☐

2. You looked at your watch and realized you have 30 minutes to wait before the bus arrives. Draw the hands on the clock to show what time it is on your watch.

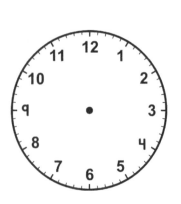

It is _____

(Write the time)

Part 2

You purchased the tickets below for your bus rides to visit your grandma. You will need a total of three of these tickets.

1. If 1 child's ticket = $60, how much will you pay for three tickets?
Show your working in the box below.

General Instructions: Read carefully, then complete each task.

TASK 7:

This task has two parts: Part 1 has three questions and Part 2 has two questions.

FOOD RUN

Felipe observed four sets of food on a table. Help him to identify each set by completing the table below.

FOOD	NAME	NUMERAL (Amount)	NUMBER NAME

Part 1

1. Which set does not have an even number of food?

    _____

2. Which food does not belong in the set?

    _____

3. Give reason for your answer.

    _____

    _____

    _____

Part 2

Scale 1   **Scale 2**   **Scale 3**

1. Observe the scales then use a tick (✓) to indicate whether the statements are True or False.

STATEMENT	TRUE	FALSE
The items on scale 2 are balanced		
On scale 1, the burger is heavier than the fruits and vegetable.		
The items on scale 3 are equal		
On scale 2, the apple is lighter than the sandwich.		

2. Have fun using your crayons to show the following: half, quarter and whole.

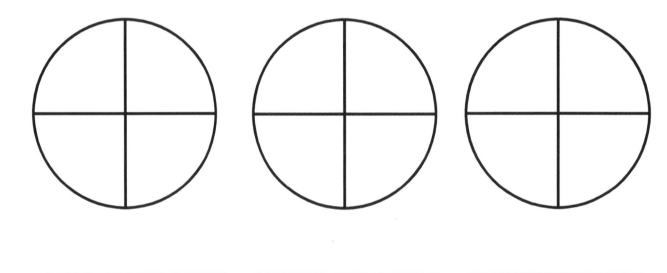

_____   _____   _____

General Instructions: Read carefully, then complete each task.

TASK 8:

This task has two parts: Part 1 has two questions and Part 2 has three questions.

Nick's 7ᵗʰ Birthday Party

Nick is celebrating his 7ᵗʰ Birthday with his friends and family. He is looking for the different shapes he will see at his party. Nick already knows that his birthday cake is in the shape of a cuboid.

Part 1

Below is a picture of Nick's birthday cake.

I.   Select which **TWO** statements below are **true** about Nick's cake.

The cake has six faces.

The edges of the cake are the same lengths.

The cake has rectangular faces.

On Nick's gift table the following gifts were seen.

2.   Based on the picture of Nick's gifts above place a tick (✓) to say if the statements below are **TRUE** or **FALSE**.

STATEMENT	TRUE	FALSE
All the gifts are solids.		
Most of Nick's gifts look like cubes and cuboids.		
There are 3 triangle shaped gifts.		
The edges of the gifts will not allow them to roll.		

Part 2

Nick burst the piñata as seen in the picture. A lot of candies fell on the ground. His friends Paula and Sean counted the number of candies they got.

Hurray!! I got 12 of my favourite candies.

Lucky you! I got 7 candies.

I.   Based on the information above:

Paula got _____ candies and Sean got _____ candies.

2.   Is it **TRUE** or **FALSE that** Sean collected the **greater** number of candies? Place a tick (✓) to show your answer.

TRUE ☐   FALSE ☐

3.   In the box below, draw the number of candies that represents the **greater** amount.

General Instructions: Read carefully, then complete each task.

TASK 9:

This task has two parts: Part 1 has six questions and Part 2 has four questions.

Part 1

Colin is a Grade one student at the Happy Days' Elementary school. Colin's mother, Mary, always says it's very important to carry the tools you need to school. Therefore, every Monday morning Mary puts 6 pencils, 3 books, 2 erasers and a sharpener in Colin's bag pack.

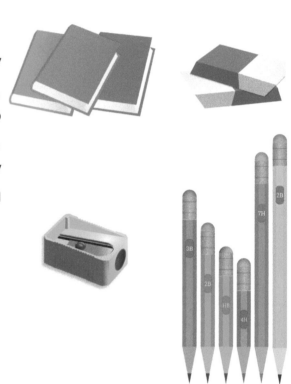

1. If you double the amount of books in Colin's bag, how many books would he have?

    _____

2. Write the number name for your answer.

    _____

3. How many tools did Colin take to school on Monday? Show your working.

4. Which colour pencil is the longest?

_____

5. If Colin gave a pencil to his friend John, what is the total number of books and pencils left? Show your working.

6. Write the number name for your answer.

_____

Part 2

1. Colin was given the following table to fill in the missing numerals. Help Colin to correctly complete his tasks.

1		3		5		7		9	
11		13		15		17		19	
21		23		25		27		29	

2. What is the largest number on the completed table?

_____

3. How many groups of tens can you get from your answer?

_____

4. If you had another row on the number table, which numeral would you be expected to fill in first? Give reason for your answer.

Glossary

WORD	MEANINGS
<	Less than
=	Is equal to/the same
>	Greater than
Activities	Special actions.
Add	Combining numbers to make a larger number.
Balance	A balance is a type of scale used to show how heavy or light something is.
Calendar	This is a chart showing a year divided into months, weeks and days.
Capacity	The most amount something contains.
Centimetre (cm)	We use centimetre for measuring short lengths or distances.
Circle	The shadow of the sphere is called a circle.
Clock	A device for showing the time.
Cube	An object with six equal square faces.
Cuboid	A geometric solid whose 6 faces are rectangles.
Even Number	A number divisible by two.
Fraction	A numerical quantity not a whole.
Grams	We weigh light objects using grams.
Half	One of two equal parts that together make up a whole.
Heavy	of great weight
Hour Hand	Tells the hours.
Kilogram	We weigh heavy objects using the kilogram measurement.
Length	How long an object is
Light	not heavy
Litre	We measure liquids using litres.
Metre	The metre is used for measuring larger objects or long distances.

WORD	MEANINGS
Minute Hand	Tells the minutes.
Odd Number	A number not divisible by two.
Ordinal Number	A number that tells the position of a person or thing.
Pattern	An arrangement of repeated parts.
Pictogram	A chart where symbols or pictures are used to represent values.
Place Value	Putting numbers in their correct places.
Quarter	One of four equal parts of something.
Rectangle	An oblong shape with four straight sides and four right angles.
Scale	A weighing machine.
Schedule	A list of things to be done at a particular time.
Set	A number of things or people grouped together.
Set, Empty	A set that has no members in it.
Sphere	A round, solid figure, every point on the surface is equally distant from the centre.
Square	A geometric figure with four equal sides and four right angles.
Subtract	To take one quantity away from another.
Sum	The result of the addition of numbers.
Tally charts	Charts that are used to show important information.
Tape Measure	A tape marked off in centimetres used for measuring.
Temperature	The hotness or coldness of something.
Thermometer	An instrument for measuring how hot or cold someone or something is.
Triangle	A geometric figure with three sides and three angles.
Zero	means nothing.

LET'S LEARN OUR COLOURS IN SPANISH

LOS COLORES
(The Colours)

blanco white

negro **black**

rojo red

amarillo yellow

marrón **brown**

verde **green**

azul **blue**

Counting Chart

1	2	3	4	5	6	7	8	9	10
11	12	13	14	15	16	17	18	19	20
21	22	23	24	25	26	27	28	29	30
31	32	33	34	35	36	37	38	39	40
41	42	43	44	45	46	47	48	49	50
51	52	53	54	55	56	57	58	59	60
61	62	63	64	65	66	67	68	69	70
71	72	73	74	75	76	77	78	79	80
81	82	83	84	85	86	87	88	89	90
91	92	93	94	95	96	97	98	99	100

CPSIA information can be obtained
at www.ICGtesting.com
Printed in the USA
LVHW071919170622
721556LV00019B/402